Mixed
Methods
Research

BLOOMSBURY RESEARCH METHODS

Edited by Mark Elliot and Jessica Nina Lester

The Bloomsbury Research Methods series provides authoritative introductions to key and emergent research methods across a range of disciplines.

Each book introduces the key elements of a particular method and/ or methodology and includes examples of its application. Written in an accessible style by leading experts in the field, this series is an innovative pedagogical and research resource.

Also available in the series

Qualitative Longitudinal Research, Bren Neale
Rhythmanalysis, Dawn Lyon
Quantitative Longitudinal Data Analysis, Vernon Gayle and
    Paul Lambert
GIS, Nick Bearman
Diary Method, Ruth Bartlett and Christine Milligan
Inclusive Research, Melanie Nind
Community Studies, Graham Crow
Embodied Inquiry, Jennifer Leigh and Nicole Brown

Forthcoming in the series

Qualitative Interviewing, 2nd edition, Rosalind Edwards and
    Janet Holland
Vignette Research, Evi Agostini, Michael Schratz and Irma Eloff
Anecdote Research, Hans Karl Peterlini and Gabriele Rathgeb
Statistical Modelling in R, Kevin Ralston, Vernon Gayle,
    Roxanne Connelly and Chris Playford

Mixed Methods Research

Research Methods

DONNA M. MERTENS

BLOOMSBURY ACADEMIC
LONDON • NEW YORK • OXFORD • NEW DELHI • SYDNEY

BLOOMSBURY ACADEMIC
Bloomsbury Publishing Plc
50 Bedford Square, London, WC1B 3DP, UK
1385 Broadway, New York, NY 10018, USA
29 Earlsfort Terrace, Dublin 2, Ireland

BLOOMSBURY, BLOOMSBURY ACADEMIC and the Diana logo
are trademarks of Bloomsbury Publishing Plc

First published in Great Britain 2023

Series design by Charlotte James
Cover image © shuoshu / iStock

A catalogue record for this book is available from the British Library.

A catalog record for this book is available from the Library of Congress.

ISBN: HB: 978-1-3502-7099-2
           PB: 978-1-3502-7098-5
         ePDF: 978-1-3502-7100-5
        eBook: 978-1-3502-7318-4

Series: Bloomsbury Research Methods

Typeset by Integra Software Services Pvt. Ltd.
Printed and bound in Great Britain

To find out more about our authors and books visit www.bloomsbury.com
and sign up for our newsletters.

CONTENTS

FIGURES

TABLES

SERIES FOREWORD

The idea behind this book series is a simple one: to provide concise and accessible introductions to frequently used research methods and to current issues in research methodology. Books in the series have been written by experts in their fields with a brief to write about their subject for a broad audience.

The series has been developed through a partnership between Bloomsbury and the UK's National Centre for Research Methods (NCRM). The original "what is" series sprang from the eponymous strand at NCRM's popular Research Methods Festivals which began in 2004 and moved online in 2021 for its ninth run.

This relaunched series reflects changes in the research landscape, embracing research methods innovation and interdisciplinarity. Methodological innovation is the order of the day, and the books provide updates to the latest developments whilst still maintaining an emphasis on accessibility to a wide audience. The format allows researchers who are new to a field to gain an insight into its key features, while also providing a useful update on recent developments for people who have had some prior acquaintance with it. All readers should find it helpful to be taken through the discussion of key terms, the history of how the method or methodological issue has developed, and the assessment of the strengths and possible weaknesses of the approach through analysis of illustrative examples.

This book is devoted to the vital topic of mixed methods. The aforesaid expansion of inter-, cross-, and trans-disciplinarity has made it important for all researchers to be at least conversant with research approaches outside of their methodological comfort zone. Another step on from there is the practice of mixed methods. However, effectively combining methods is an exemplar of the adage "the whole is more than the sum of the parts" and mixed methods practice requires additional skills and insights beyond merely understanding each of the methods in question. In this book, Donna Mertens frames the whole of her exposition around this point: mixed methods should be integrative. Mertens develops her narrative by tracing the origins and early history of mixed methods, drawing from interviews that she conducted with key scholars who were involved in the earliest days of mixed methods research practices and perspectives. This is a particularly unique feature of the book, as there are few accounts of how mixed methods came to be and the reasons that drove and shaped its development.

Mertens foregrounds the question of how researchers might adapt methodologies to address increasingly complex programs of research in ways that might even lead to improving and changing current practice and social dilemmas. Concomitantly, the book highlights the ways in which mixed methods research can be designed across a range of paradigms and orientations (Post-Positivist, Constructivist, Pragmatic, Transformative, and Indigenous paradigms, along with the meta-paradigm, Dialectical Pluralism) – that is, there is no one preferred way to design a mixed methods research study.

What is emphasized throughout is that mixed methods research serves to capture the layered and complex aspects of a phenomenon of interest in a way that a foundation is laid to identify key solutions and pathways toward change. Generative case studies are provided throughout to bring this nuanced methodological practice to life for the reader.

The books in this series cannot provide information about their subject matter down to a fine level of detail, but they equip readers with a powerful sense of reasons why it deserves to be taken seriously and, it is hoped, with the enthusiasm to put that knowledge into practice.

Jessica Nina Lester and Mark Elliot

CHAPTER ONE

Definition of Mixed Methods and its Emergence as a Methodological Approach

---

Objectives

1. Define mixed methods research.
2. Identify key historical moments in the development of mixed methods research.
3. Recognize the characteristics of the philosophical frameworks used in mixed methods research.

Mixed methods research is an expanding area of interest for researchers across many disciplines because researchers face many complex problems that challenge understanding and, at time, seem to defy solutions. These complexities are present in disciplines that involve understanding human behavior and promoting improvements in the quality of life, such as education, and the health and social sciences. In the educational sector, inequities in access to quality education and disparities in academic achievement based on gender, race/ethnicity, abilities, language, and socioeconomic status are acknowledged problems in many parts of the world. How can researchers adapt their methodologies to address such complex problems in ways that lead to improved school climate, address power hierarchies, and challenge discriminatory practices in order to increase equity and improve achievement in schooling? Many researchers have come to the conclusion that a single method is not sufficient to address problems of this magnitude and complexity. They have turned to the use of mixed methods research in order to collect data that can capture the multiple aspects of a phenomenon and provide a basis for the development of solutions that have the potential to create needed changes. For example, Garnett and colleagues chose to use a mixed methods approach to explore how researchers can reach a more accurate understanding of the problem of school inequities and support the development of interventions that lead to structural and systemic changes for the most marginalized students (Garnett, Smight, Kevick, Ballysigh, Moore and Gonell 2019).

This book begins with a brief history of the emergence of this field and includes numerous examples to illustrate its application in different disciplines and geographic areas (see Table 1.1). The voices of thought leaders in the mixed methods field are featured as they share their experiences and practices, innovative designs, preparation of mixed methods researchers, and how mixed methods research can contribute to a more just and equitable future. Mixed methods approaches offer researchers an exciting opportunity to explore new combinations of methods in diverse contexts. Before getting into design options, let's clarify what is mixed methods research.

What Is Mixed Methods Research?

The answer to the question of what is mixed methods could be quite simplistic: it is the inclusion of both quantitative and qualitative methods in a single study or a sequence of studies. However, if the answer to that question were that simplistic, you would not need to read the rest of this book. Many mixed methods researchers agree that inclusion of both quantitative and qualitative methods is fundamental for this approach (Creswell and Plano Clark 2011; Johnson, Onwuegbuzie and Turner 2007; Mertens 2018). However, there is also agreement that the quantitative and qualitative methods need to be integrated and used to achieve a better level of understanding than would be possible through the use of a single method or even the use of several quantitative or several qualitative methods in a single study. The *Journal of Mixed Methods Research* (2021) provides this definition of mixed methods research: "collecting and analyzing data, integrating the findings, and drawing inferences using both qualitative and quantitative approaches or methods ... [that] explicitly integrate the quantitative and qualitative aspects of the study."

Moran-Ellis and colleagues (2006) recognize the importance of integration in mixed methods studies thusly:

> 'integration' denotes a specific relationship between two or more methods where the different methods ... are inter-meshed with each other in pursuit of the goal of 'knowing more'. We describe the greatest level of integration as integrated methods, in which the inter-meshing occurs from conceptualization onwards to the final reporting of the research.
>
> (p. 51)

Mixed methods researchers work from different sets of assumptions; these sets of assumptions are called paradigms. They serve to guide researchers' thinking and choices. Mixed methods researchers emphasize the importance of being consciously aware of the paradigmatic assumptions that guide their methodological choices. The understanding of the frameworks of assumptions to guide mixed methods researchers is diverse and complex, hence the need for a book that explores the different approaches to mixed methods and illustrates these different approaches in order to have a fuller understanding of the answer to the question: What is mixed methods research? The concept of paradigms is introduced later in this chapter and expanded upon in Chapter 2.

History of Mixed Methods Research

Researchers can come to a better understanding of the meaning of mixed methods research by reviewing a brief history of the use of both quantitative and qualitative methods and the emergence of this methodology (Maxwell 2016). Researchers were laying the groundwork for what is now called mixed methods research as early as the 1800s when both quantitative and qualitative methods were used to study poverty in Europe (Le Play 1855, cited in Hesse

Biber 2010). In 1899, W. E. B. Du Bois used both quantitative and qualitative methods in his landmark study, *The Philadelphia Negro,* that combined ethnography, historical analysis, and descriptive statistics. Campbell and Fiske (1956) were early pioneers in promoting the use of mixed methods through their development of the multitrait, multimethod matrix that included both quantitative and qualitative methods to strengthen research conclusions. And, Ray Paul combined qualitative methods of ethnographic observations, interviews, archival research, and visual methods with quantitative surveys in his study of the division of labor in 1984. Allen Bryman published *Quantity and Quality in Social Research* (1988) and Julia Brannen (1992) edited a volume entitled *Mixing Methods: Qualitative and Quantitative Research.*

So, why are we talking about mixed methods research as an emerging methodology? Despite evidence that researchers have been using both quantitative and qualitative methods in their studies for centuries, Maxwell (2016) suggests that mixed methods research only emerged as a "distinct and self-conscious strategy" (p. 12) in the 1980s and 1990s. While quantitative and qualitative methods have been combined in studies in the distant past, it was not until the late twentieth century that the term *mixed methods* began to appear in the literature (Fetters 2016). Fetters describes the emergence of this conscious development of an approach called mixed methods as follows:

> The idea of intentional linking of qualitative research with quantitative research with clear intentions for integration not only in an applied way, but also through systematic methodological approaches emerged rather simultaneously. Through writings illustrating various techniques and procedures, these modern-day innovators began systematically considering the possibilities for linking the qualitative and the quantitative together.
>
> (16)

The development of mixed methods as a formal approach received a huge boost when the first International Mixed Methods Congress was held at Cambridge University in 2005 (Mertens 2013). In an interview I conducted on July 11, 2021, with the convener for this ground-breaking conference, Tessa Muncy, she said she was motivated to start this movement because of her own experiences when she directed her students' research programs at Cambridge University and witnessed a lack of opportunities in professional organizations to talk explicitly about mixed methods. She said that she and her students were frustrated because there seemed to be no outlet for mixed methods studies. She went to several conferences that were focused on qualitative methods and healthcare and noticed that some of the speakers were promoting the use of mixed methods. She was motivated to organize a mixed methods conference in Cambridge in 2005. She described the process as follows:

> I started with a small list of people to contact; many of them said they would help to make it happen. I don't know how we did it really. We just got the message out there. We started with no mechanism to do it, no email system, no Facebook, we were going from nothing. We were absolutely staggered; we thought we could break even with 50 attendees. In the end, in July 2005, we had too many people to sit in the biggest room available to us; people sat on the stairs. People came from all over the world. We already knew by lunchtime of the first day that if we were going to carry on, we would need to go somewhere bigger because we had seriously underestimated the interest. All anybody said was, you have to keep this going. It met all my tick boxes, it was multidisciplinary, it was a true range of mixed methods, and they were the loveliest people. For the following conferences, we just had to ask people and they agreed to come.

When I asked Tessa, "Why do you think people were so eager to be involved?" she replied:

> That is a good question. They were certainly hungry to be involved. I think it was because it gave permission to talk about the whole spectrum of what they were doing. One participant, a general practitioner of medicine in the UK, said, "I am so fed up with going to medical conferences and they only want to hear about the RCT [randomized controlled trial] bit." In order to talk about qualitative aspects of her work, she had to go to another conference and they are only interested in that. She said her study was more than the two parts. It's the whole thing. And in my heart, I believe that's why people wanted the mixed methods forum. Because they could be whole. At first people just

wanted to talk about their studies, but it evolved. They began to expand, looking at the pitfalls like how do you get over when one method starts to dominate or at the end you might end up with a different research question than when you started. That's what the conference became: a discussion about how to mix things. The mixed methods community is just an amazing community that I feel privileged to be part of.

This first conference was followed by annual meetings for several years in Cambridge, with a move to Leeds University in 2009. It continued in that venue until 2012 with one exception, a mixed methods conference was held in Baltimore Maryland (USA) in 2010 in conjunction with Johns Hopkins University (Mertens 2014). Informal discussions at these conferences raised the idea of starting a professional association that was devoted to mixed methods research. Those informal discussions blossomed into a steering committee that developed objectives, bylaws, and completed the administrative aspects of creating a legal entity. The Mixed Methods International Research Association was launched in 2013. The inaugural MMIRA Global Conference was held in Boston, Massachusetts, under the stewardship of Sharlene Hesse Biber. This was followed by additional international conferences, regional conferences, and the establishment of regional affiliates of MMIRA.

The mission of MMIRA is described as follows:

... to create an international community to promote interdisciplinary mixed methods research. The mission of the Association is to engage with the international community to support mixed methods research, which broadly includes the following: mixing/combining/integrating quantitative and/or qualitative methods, epistemologies, axiologies, and stakeholder perspectives and standpoints.

MMIRA seeks to engage with a broad set of approaches in the service of understanding complex social, behavioral, health, educational, and political concerns related to the human condition and natural world. Our vision includes bringing together diverse communities of scholars, students, practitioners, policymakers, citizens, and other stakeholders, with the goals of expanding knowledge and producing social betterment and social and global justice.

(MMIRA.org July 2021)

Another significant development in the mixed methods field was the publication of the *Journal of Mixed Methods Research's (JMMR)* first issue in 2007 under the editorial leadership of Abbas Tashakkori and John Creswell, who were followed by editors Donna Mertens, Manfred Max Bergman, Dawn Freshwater, Michael Fetters, and Jose Molina-Azorin. The journal's website contains this description:

> The *Journal of Mixed Methods Research (JMMR)* is an innovative, quarterly, interdisciplinary, international publication that focuses on empirical methodological articles, methodological/theoretical articles, and commentaries about mixed methods research across the social, behavioral, health, and human sciences. The scope includes delineating where mixed methods research may be used most effectively, illuminating design and procedure issues, and determining the logistics of conducting mixed methods research. (https://journals.sagepub.com/home/mmr, July 2021)

JMMR provides a space for the publication of studies and theoretical and methodological papers that are explicitly focused on the use of mixed methods. One of the journal's many strengths is that it is inclusive of diverse views of framing and conducting mixed methods research. Readers find empirical articles as well as theoretical and philosophical articles that explore frameworks that provide guidance to conducting rigorous mixed methods studies. These philosophical frameworks are briefly introduced near the end of this chapter with an expansion of explanation and illustration in Chapter 2.

JMMR is the only journal that has a mission to publish mixed methods articles that specifically focus on this methodology. However, other journals in the social, behavioral, business, and health sciences have changed their editorial policies to seek out or encourage mixed methods research studies (Fetters and Molina-Azorin 2021b).

Mixed Methods Guidance Is Increasing

The mixed methods research community is witnessing an increase in guidance provided by professional associations, funders, government agencies, non profit organizations, and publishers on the use of mixed methods (Fetters and Molina-Azorin 2021b). For example, the World Bank (Bamberger, Rao and Woolcock 2010) and the United States Agency for International Development (USAID 2013) published reports that provide guidance for mixed methods research in international development. A major funder of behavioral and health-related research around the world, the National Institutes of Health Office of Behavioral and Social Sciences, published best practices guidance for mixed methods research for researchers seeking funds from their organization (Creswell et al. 2011). United Nations organizations, including the Special Program for Research and Training in Tropical Diseases (TDR), United Nations Children's Fund (UNICEF), the United Nations Development Programme (UNDP), and the World Health Organization (WHO), recognized mixed methods as a fundamental methodology for conducting implementation research (TDR 2021). No specific guidelines were found for mixed methods research in the UK, except for the government's guidelines related to the use of mixed methods for evaluating digital health products (Public Health England 2020).

Foundations have also provided guidance for mixed methods research (Fetters and Molina-Azorin 2021b). For example, the FoodRisc Resource Centre in the European Union provides guidance for the use of mixed methods research concerning the consumer perspective in food safety issues (FoodRisc Resource Centre 2016). Other organizations have developed mixed methods publication standards, including the Joanna Briggs Institute in Australia that focuses on healthcare and the American Psychological Association (Levitt et al. 2018).

Philosophical Foundations for Mixed Methods Research

The mixed methods community enjoys a richness of many different philosophical frameworks that can inform their work. I use the terminology of research paradigms to depict the set of philosophical assumptions that guide thinking and decision-making in mixed methods research (Mertens 2018). Thomas Kuhn (1962) introduced the term paradigm in his influential book *The Structure of Scientific Revolution*. He wrote that as new assumptions emerged to inform scientific research, they replaced the prevailing sets of assumptions. He called this a paradigm shift. Guba and Lincoln (1989; 2005) rejected the idea that newer paradigms replaced older paradigms, especially in social research. They were writing in response to the paradigm wars in which researchers argued whether quantitative or qualitative research was best. Their landmark contribution was to assert that the question was not about which method was best; rather, the more legitimate question is about the assumptions that guide methodological choices. To this end, they identified four sets of assumptions that describe paradigmatic frameworks for social research:

- The axiological assumption is about the nature of values and ethics.

- The ontological assumption is about the nature of reality.

- The epistemological assumption is about the nature of knowledge and the relationship between the researcher and participants.

- The methodological assumption is about the nature of systematic inquiry.

The use of the paradigmatic frameworks allowed researchers to get past the arguments about which method, quantitative or qualitative, was better and focus on how their assumptions informed methodological choices. Five paradigms and one meta-paradigm are described in the mixed methods literature (Mertens 2018; 2020a). In 1989, Guba and Lincoln focused on the assumptions of two paradigms: Post-positivism and Constructivism. With the emergence of mixed methods, Tashakkori and Teddlie (2003) identified the Pragmatic paradigm as a framework that avoided concerns that researchers could not mix assumptions from the two previously dominant paradigms. Mertens (2020a) added a fourth paradigm called the Transformative paradigm that provides a framework for research that explicitly addresses issues of social, economic, and environmental justice and human rights. Chilisa (2020) and Cram (2016) identified a fifth paradigm: the Indigenous paradigm that is rooted in the worldviews of Indigenous people. Greene and Hall (2010) and Johnson and Stefurak (2013) suggest that a meta-paradigm called Dialectical Pluralism would provide a framework for working across paradigms while maintaining the integrity of each paradigm's assumptions.

In mixed methods research, the design possibilities are endless and can incorporate many different approaches. The concept of paradigms in research is used to illustrate how different assumptions lead researchers to select different methodologies, resulting in the use of different research designs. Paradigms are made up of sets of assumptions about the nature of ethics, reality, knowledge, and systematic inquiry. In the mixed methods literature, five philosophical paradigms and Dialectical Pluralism provide frameworks to guide thinking and pathways to different choices in a mixed methods study. Table 1.1 displays the most basic description of each paradigm; these descriptions are overly simplistic and should serve as a guiding framework for understanding the characteristics of mixed methods research examples presented in Chapter 2. The descriptions are elaborated in the specific parts of Chapter 2 in which a paradigm is discussed along with illustrations of their application. You will find a listing of the sample studies in Table 1.2 to guide you as you read through Chapter 2. The range of studies is quite diverse representing many different countries and topics, with most focusing on education, health, policy analysis, and social issues such as economic development, environmental justice, children's care and play, and interpersonal violence.

TABLE 1.1 Basic Description of Paradigms in Mixed Methods

Post-Positivism: Mixed methods can be used; the dominant methods include the collection of quantitative data with qualitative data playing a supplemental role. Priority is given to experimental designs.
Constructivism: Mixed methods can be used; the dominant methods are qualitative with quantitative data playing a supplemental role. Priority is given to designs that are based on constructivist theory.
Pragmatism: The use of mixed methods is deemed to be essential if the research questions are best answered using both quantitative and qualitative data.

Transformative: The use of mixed methods is most commonly used because of the need to be inclusive of a broad range of stakeholders and to contribute to positive, sustainable transformative change.

Indigenous: Mixed methods are used with a cultural lens that reflects Indigenous worldviews. These views can differ for different Indigenous groups but are rooted in their history and connection with the land.

Dialectical Pluralism: The researcher operates with two or more different paradigms and maintains the integrity of the assumptions of the chosen paradigms. Mixing occurs when the different paradigms are put into conversation with each other.

TABLE 1.2 Sample Mixed Methods Studies

Post-positivism and mixed methods		
Study	**Design**	**Topic/location**
Kong, Yaacov, and Ariffin (2018)	Quasi-experimental design	Environmental education in Malaysia
Gibbs, Washington, Willan, Ntini, Khumalo, Mbatha, Sikweyiya, Shai, Chirwa, Strauss, Ferrari, and Jewkes (2017)	Randomized control trial experimental design	Intimate partner violence in South Africa
Rees-Evans and Pevalin (2017)	Single-group, pre-, post-, and follow-up mixed methods study	Teacher stress in England
Constructivism and mixed methods		
Harding, Sullivan, Yong, and Crutch (2021)	Ethnographic design with psychometric measurement	Negotiating dementia in England
Cheek, Lipschitz, Abrams, Vago, and Nakamura, (2015)	Critically reflective dialogue and document review, interviews and a battery of tests and measurements	Mindfulness training in the United States

Kacperski, Ulloa, and Hall (2019)	Phenomenological study with quantitative surveys and quantitizing of qualitative data	Use of imagery by athletes in Canada
Pragmatism and mixed methods		
Bogaert, De Martelaer, Deforche, Clarys, and Zinzen (2015)	Parallel mixed methods design with standardized questionnaire and focus groups	Describing physical exercise as a means to stress reduction for teachers in Belgium
Shannon, Borron, Kurtz, and Weaver (2021)	Participatory mixed methods approach with concept mapping	Stimulate discussion of policy change around food security issues in the United States
Khadaroo and MacCallum (2021)	Embedded design with a two-phase approach: quantitative survey and semi-structured interviews	Compare single-child families with multi-child families in England
Holtrop, Potworowski, Green, and Fetters (2019)	Convergent mixed methods design: Quantitative data extant database: "big data"; qualitative data collected in two different tracks with integration at the end	Chronic health conditions for elderly people in the United States to inform insurers and healthcare administrators
Transformative paradigm and mixed methods		
Miller (2020)	Evolving design with advocacy organizations including quantitative checklist and legislative analysis; transcripts from support meetings; and interviews	Transformation of health care for gay and bi-sexual men and trans-women in Cameroon; capacity development in research skills
Garnett, Smith, Kervick, Ballysingh, Moore, and Gonell (2019)	Building relationships; contextual analysis; extant data analysis; meetings with students; interviews; surveys	Changing disciplinary practices to address inequities in schools for racial minorities and students with disabilities in the United States

Menon and Hartz-Karp (2020)	Forming coalition; interviews; quantitative survey; action research through public deliberations	Change public policy on use of space to create safer streets and increase environmental health in India
Sullivan, Derrett, Paul, Beaver, and Stace (2014)	Community-based research team (co-researchers); quantitative surveys and qualitative interviews	Build capacity of persons with spinal cord injuries to conduct research and change policies to increase support for this community in New Zealand
Indigenous paradigm and mixed methods		
Arko-Achemfuor, Romm and Serolong (2019); McIntyre-Mills, Karel, Arko-Achemfuor, Romm, and Serolong (2019)	Build relationships with village chief and residents; contextual analysis of literacy levels and farming practices; interventions evolved informed by data	Increase literacy levels and sustainable agricultural methods to promote economic development of South African farmers
Lucero, Wallerstein, Duran, Alegria, Greene-Moton, Israel, Kastelic, Magarati, Oetzel, Pearson, Schulz, Villegas, and White Hat (2018)	Iterative integration approach: Develop inclusive partnerships with Native American communities; community-based participatory mixed methods design; case studies followed by surveys	Implement culturally responsive interventions to improve health care in the Native American community; change policies and practices; reduce health disparities
Henwood and Henwood (2011)	Build relationships with Indigenous community and livestock farmers; prioritize Indigenous values; contextual analysis	Restoration of a lake used by livestock farmers and the Māori community; change farming practices to be ecologically sound; improve water quality in New Zealand

Bird-Naytowhow, Hatala, Pearl, Judge, and Sjoblom (2017)	Prioritize spirituality; build relationships with tribal council and youth; contextual analysis; qualitative data (photo voice and interviews); quantitative data (extant data on health inequities)	Directly benefit youth in building research capacity and reduce inequities in terms of risk of alcoholism, drug use, and suicide in Indigenous youth in Canada
Wilson and Cram (2018)	Set up Māori ethical review board; created predictive risk model based on "big data"; qualitative collaborative inquiry with Māori community	Prevent the use of an algorithm that would over-identify Māori children as being "at risk"; make visible the historic roots of over-representation in the system in New Zealand
Dialectical Pluralism and mixed methods		
Shim, Johnson, Bradt, and Gasson (2021)	Grounded theory and quasi-experimental design	Pain management in movement therapy (dance) in the United States
Bhuyan and Zhang (2020)	Two-phase mixed methods: Interviews and children's drawings followed by systematic observations and quantitative analysis of maps and GIS data	Describe play preferences of children in Bangladesh
Leal, Engebretson, Cohen, Fernandez-Esquer, Lopez, Wangyal, and Chaoul (2018)	Randomized control trial experimental design and constructivist written narratives	Compare experiences of cancer patients who participated in yoga with a control group in the United States

Summary

Mixed methods is emerging as an important approach to research because it involves gathering both quantitative and qualitative data and integrating that data to reach a better understanding than would be possible with one data collection method. Many advances in mixed methods research have occurred in the past couple of decades, including in publications in journals, guidance from professional associations, and recommendations from funding agencies. The assumptions that guide methodological choices, or paradigms, are important because researchers will develop different mixed methods designs based on their assumptions.

Questions for Further Thinking:

1. For what kinds of research problems do you think mixed methods are appropriate?
2. Why is it important to understand the history of mixed methods?
3. What information can you learn from the websites for the Mixed Methods International Research Association (mmira.org) and the *Journal of Mixed Methods Research* (https://journals.sagepub.com/home/mmr)?
4. What are the dominant methodologies in your discipline? How frequently are mixed methods used in your discipline?

CHAPTER TWO

Evolving Paradigms in Mixed Methods: Case Studies

Objectives

1. Identify the characteristics of the Post-Positivist, Constructivist, Pragmatic, Transformative, and Indigenous paradigms, along with the meta-paradigm, Dialectical Pluralism.
2. Analyze the characteristics of case studies to determine their application of the assumptions from the five paradigms and Dialectical Pluralism.
3. Contemplate the importance of philosophical assumptions in making methodological choices.

The Post-Positivist, Constructivist, Pragmatic, Transformative, and Indigenous paradigms, along with one meta-paradigm, Dialectical Pluralism, are used to guide the thinking of mixed methods researchers. I use paradigms to frame how to do mixed methods research because they help researchers clarify the assumptions that guide their methodological choices. The specific assumptions for each paradigm are presented in this chapter, along with examples of research studies that demonstrate the influence of the paradigm's assumptions on all aspects of a mixed methods research study from the generation of the research questions to the design, implementation, and use of the research findings. I provide a graphic display of one mixed methods design for each of the frameworks to help you visualize how the assumptions influence design decisions.

Mixed Methods and the Post-Positivist Paradigm

Rationale for use of mixed methods with the Post-Positivist paradigm is provided by White (2013) based on the importance of answering the research question: "What difference did the intervention make?" (61). He argues that a randomized control trial (RCT) design is the best approach to answer this question because it adheres to the assumptions of the Post-Positivist paradigm (see Table 2.1). RCTs consist of an experimental group that receives a treatment (the independent variable) and a control group that does not get the experimental treatment. When members of the two groups have been randomly assigned (each has an equal chance to be in either group), the researcher assumes that any extraneous

TABLE 2.1 Philosophical Assumptions of the Post-Positivist Paradigm

Axiology: Adherence to institutional review guidelines for ethical practice, usually including respect for privacy, informed consent, minimizing harm, and justice in the form of equal opportunity to participate in and benefit from the research.
Ontology: The assumption is made that there is a reality that exists and that researchers can measure it, albeit not perfectly, but within a specified level of probability.
Epistemology: The researcher should be objective and not allow personal biases to influence the research findings. To this end, the researcher should manipulate an intervention and measure in a dispassionate manner. The researcher is considered to be the expert, and knowledge from the experts is highly valued.
Methodology: Quantitative methods dominate; qualitative methods can be supplemental; the work is decontextualized in order to control for extraneous variables.

variables (e.g., age, previous knowledge) are controlled, thus supporting the conclusion that any differences between the groups on the dependent variable (the expected effects of the intervention) are due to the experimental treatment. The differences in outcomes using this design are measured quantitatively. This design reflects the ontological assumption that there is a reality (quantity of dependent variable) that can be measured within a specified level of error, given that no measurement is perfect in social research. Reflecting the Post-Positivist epistemological assumption, the quantitative measurement limits the researcher's interactions with the participants, and this is taken as evidence of the researcher's objectivity. The researcher assumes that they do not influence participants because everyone responds to the same quantitative measurement.

Quantitative methods tend to dominate in Post-Positivist mixed methods research. However, researchers typically have additional questions beyond the one about effectiveness, and this is where mixed methods enters the Post-Positivist's practice. White (2013) recommends the use of both quantitative and qualitative data to answer questions such as: What influences the participation rate in intervention studies? What are the reasons that people drop out of studies? What conditions need to be considered when planning data collection (e.g., weather conditions, religious holidays)? To what extent was the intervention implemented as planned? Data to answer these types of questions can be both quantitative and qualitative, and they can provide insights into the design of the intervention, data collection methods, and interpretation of data.

Sometimes random assignment to experimental and control groups is not possible. However, it might be possible to have comparison groups that come from two different locations that are not randomly assigned to conditions (e.g., schools, classrooms, villages). When this adaptation is used, it is called a quasi-experimental design (Mertens 2020a). The quasi-experimental design has many of the benefits of an experimental design, but questions can arise as to the comparability of the two groups being compared. The use of mixed methods is advantageous in these circumstances in order to investigate differences that might pre-exist between the groups such as being more geographically isolated or having differential access to resources (e.g., food, clean water, employment, health care). Several case studies of mixed methods studies that were framed with the Post-Positivist assumptions are presented to illustrate application using this framework.

Case Studies of Mixed Methods with the Post-Positivist Paradigm

Mixed Methods Post-Positivist Case Study #1: Environmental Education

A Post-Positivist mixed methods study is illustrated by Kong, Yaacov, and Ariffin (2018) in their study of the development and effectiveness of an intervention to improve environmental education for primary education students in Malaysia. A team of research architects conducted the study and published it to demonstrate the usefulness of mixed methods with a quasi-experimental research design in planning and designing architectural interventions in the classroom. They worked from the premise that the design of a learning environment can provide a tool for teaching and imparting values that support ecological literacy.

Kong and colleagues (2018) conducted a multi-phase study that included qualitative data collection in the first phase and both quantitative and qualitative data in the second phase. The qualitative phase was needed because they needed to develop design criteria to use as a basis for developing the intervention. They described their design as an exploratory sequential design (Creswell and Plano Clark 2011), indicating that qualitative data would be collected first to help develop the intervention. This would be followed by a second phase that included a quasi-experimental study with both quantitative and qualitative data collection to test the intervention effectiveness. Figure 2.1 depicts the design.

Their research questions were derived from gaps in the existing literature about environmental education (Kong et al. 2018). The first phase used a qualitative approach in order to focus on the question: "What are the design features of a 3-D textbook?" (150); they explained a 3-D textbook as the physical environment and the real-world objects within it that are used to teach topics usually

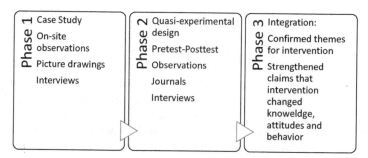

Phase 1
1 Case Study
On-site observations
Picture drawings
Interviews

Phase 2
2 Quasi-experimental design
Pretest-Posttest
Observations
Journals
Interviews

Phase 3
3 Integration:
Confirmed themes for intervention
Strengthened claims that intervention changed knowledge, attitudes and behavior

FIGURE 2.1 *Exploratory Sequential Mixed Methods Design for Environmental Education (Adapted from Kong et al. 2018).*

studied from textbooks. The study took place in a single primary school in Bali, Indonesia, that had already made a commitment to use its buildings and landscape to teach environmental education (EE). The intent was to understand the design criteria for a 3-D book from the students' point of view. Two primary qualitative data collection methods were used: on-site observation and interviews. The on-site observations yielded records of the use of indoor and outdoor spaces in the school. The outdoor observations were conducted in the garden and farming plots; the indoor observations took place in the science lab and classrooms. The researchers indicated that they used purposeful sampling to select fifth graders for in-depth interviews. The students were asked to draw two pictures to illustrate their perception of the school and how they would like it to change. These pictures formed the basis for the interviews which were open-ended. Follow-up questions were asked to elicit more information about the places the children used in the school and their typical activities in those spaces. The researchers also briefly interviewed selected teachers, administrative staff, and the school's green architect. The qualitative data were analyzed using adaptations of the constant comparison (Glaser and Strauss 1967) and grounded theory (Miles and Huberman 1994) approaches. The themes that emerged provided a guide for the development of the 3-D textbook. The researchers shared the data with a group of interdisciplinary partners, including educators, builders, and architects, to inform the development of preliminary environmental features. Input from students was sought to refine and finalize the intervention design. This first phase was purely qualitative, but it was used as a basis for development of the intervention; the second phase of the study included both quantitative and qualitative data.

Their second research question was: "Can a 3-D textbook enhance EE (environmental education) outcomes?" (Kong et al. 2018: 150). The researchers describe their rationale for a quasi-experimental design as "to test the effectiveness of the 3-D textbook by gathering numerical information and figures with statistical support to strengthen the findings from phase 1" (156–57). Their design choice was a pretest–post-test nonequivalent comparison group design (Babbie 1992). They were not able to randomly assign students to the experimental (3-D textbook) and control conditions, making them nonequivalent comparison groups. They gave both groups pre- and post-tests to determine their similarities before treatment and to document differences after treatment. They hypothesized that students who interacted with the 3-D textbook would demonstrate more changes in their environmental knowledge, attitudes, and behaviors than students who engaged in normal classroom lessons, after statistically controlling for pretest scores. The experimental group designed, built, and operated the physical model. A control group was chosen that was similar in gender, ethnicity, and academic performance. Based on the results of phase 1, the researchers designed the quantitative data collection instruments. They administered the instruments prior to the intervention and afterward. They also collected qualitative data during phase 2 to improve their interpretation of the quantitative results. The qualitative data consisted of on-site observations, personal journal entries, and follow-up interviews. Integration of the quantitative and qualitative data provided evidence of the effectiveness of the intervention along with confirmation that the themes identified in phase 1.

Kong et al.'s (2018) study demonstrates a strong mixed methods approach with the use of a quasi-experimental design typically associated with the Post-Positivist paradigm in conjunction with qualitative data to inform the development of the intervention and confirm the quantitative results on the effectiveness of the intervention. They identified their research question from existing literature – an acceptable practice but one that does not give power to the students or teachers to determine what is important to them. They also demonstrated integration of the quantitative and qualitative aspects of their study by using the qualitative data from phase one to help develop the quantitative instruments used in phase two. Another strength in their approach was that they circled back to the themes identified in the first phase when they were interpreting the results of the second phase, thus supporting their conclusion that the treatment resulted in improved environmental knowledge, attitudes, and behaviors.

Mixed Methods Post-Positivist Case Study #2: Intimate Partner Violence

Gibbs and colleagues (2017) provide another example of a quantitatively dominant mixed methods study that was designed to prevent intimate partner violence in South Africa. Their literature review indicated that men who do not have economic opportunities were more likely to perpetrate violence against women and engage in risky behaviors that are associated with HIV transmission. The researchers sought to test a hypothesis that an intervention that included addressing gender norms and economic conditions would lead to less intimate partner violence and decreased engagement in HIV-risk behaviors. They used an RCT design in which the experimental group received the independent variable: Stepping Stones and Creating a Future. The control group lived their lives as usual without interventions. (The control group members were put on a wait-list for receiving the treatment after the study was complete.) One question that might be raised is: How culturally responsive were the interventions for this population?

The researchers were not able to randomly assign individuals to experimental and control groups; instead, they randomly assigned informal settlements to these two conditions. Informal settlements are densely populated areas, usually located on under-used land or steep hillsides adjacent to urban areas that do not receive formal services such as electricity or piped-in water. The settlements are typically geographically bounded; thus, it was possible to randomly assign these settlements to experimental or control groups. This type of design is known as a cluster randomized control design. They described their study objective as follows:

The main objectives of the trial are to determine through a cluster randomized control trial (RCT) whether the combined Stepping Stones and Creating Futures interventions are effective in enabling young women and men (18–30) in informal settlements to reduce their exposure/perpetration to physical and/or sexual IPV and strengthen young women and men's livelihoods.

(369)

The dependent variables were predominately measured using quantitative scales that asked men about violent physical and sexual perpetration; women were asked about their experience of the same behaviors (Gibbs et al. 2017). Quantitative scales were also used to measure controlling behaviors and income. Controlling behaviors were assessed using a standardized scale. Participants were asked about how much money they earned in the previous month. Other standardized quantitative scales asked about depression symptoms, suicidal ideation, and satisfaction with life. These scales were administered as pre- and post-tests to both the experimental and control groups. The pretests provided baseline data; post-tests captured immediate effects, and these were followed up at six and twelve months after the intervention. The researchers do not explicitly address whether the standardized instruments were viewed as being culturally appropriate by the participants.

Mixed methods entered the picture when the researchers wanted to understand how the interventions were delivered on the ground and to gain insights into the interrelationship between gender inequalities, livelihoods, and intimate partner violence (Gibbs et al. 2017). They also wanted to capture the influence of the social context on the intervention outcomes. To this end, fieldworkers conducted interviews and engaged in participant observation throughout the duration of the implementation and the follow-up periods. The methods included focus groups and in-depth interviews with facilitators and observations in two non-randomly selected clusters. One weakness of this study was that integration of quantitative and qualitative data came only at the stage of data interpretation. A strength of the study was that the qualitative data illuminated the process of change and captured unforeseen impacts. The authors hope that the combination of two types of data will inform revisions of the intervention for future implementation. The dominance of the quantitative aspects of the study aligns with the Post-Positivist paradigm, along with the use of an RCT design.

Gibbs et al. (2017) specifically mention that they structured the study to adhere to the ethical guidelines provided by the World Medical Association *Declaration of Helsinki* (2013) and the *Belmont Report* (National Commission for the Protection of Human Subjects of Biomedical and Behavioral Research 1978). These guidelines are widely used for institutional ethical review and include "respect for person's autonomy, justice, beneficence, and non-maleficence (do no harm) in the conduct of research with human participants" (347). These align with the ethical assumption of the Post-Positivist paradigm. It is important to mention that researchers need to obtain ethical approval through the review process that their institutional home prescribes no matter what paradigm is used to structure the research. The criteria in the *Helsinki Declaration* and the *Belmont Report* are often the criteria that institutional review boards use to review proposals. As we move into other paradigmatic frameworks for mixed methods, we will see modifications or additions to what is needed for an ethical study. Adherence to these modifications or additions does not excuse the researcher from completing the institutional ethical review process.

Mixed Methods Post-Positivist Case Study #3: Student and Teacher Stress

A third mixed methods study using the Post-Positivist paradigm was conducted by Rees-Evans and Pevalin (2017) to address the stress experienced by students and teachers in England. They wanted to test a school-based intervention that was designed to improve the psychological well-being of students and staff in one high school. The intervention was a standardized program that focused on positive thinking and awareness of how this can lead to a calmer, more positive emotional state. The authors do not mention any opportunity for the teachers or students to have input as to the need for this program or to modify it to more explicitly meet their needs.

Their ethical requirements were met through approval from the school where the study was conducted and their university's ethical review board. They described their design as a single-group, pre-, post-, and follow-up mixed methods study. The quantitative changes in well-being were measured with a standardized instrument, the Friedman Well-Being Scale (FWBS), which has five subscales, before the intervention was implemented (pre), immediately after the intervention (post), and a third time at an unspecified time (follow-up). The authors assumed that this was a valid instrument for this population. Qualitative data were also collected during a follow-up period through interviews with students and staff.

Analysis of the quantitative data revealed that there was no statistically significant change on the FWBS for staff and that only two of the five subscales showed a significant change for students (Rees-Evans and Pevalin 2017). The researchers then analyzed the qualitative data; this resulted in the emergence of three themes: motivation for participating, participant personal changes, and reduction of stress. The integration of the quantitative and qualitative data occurred when the researchers used the results of the qualitative data to gain explanatory value of the quantitative results. The results were weaker than they had hoped partly because some of the staff participated with the goal of reducing their stress, while others just did so out of curiosity. Some staff and students reported that they became more aware of the power of positive thinking which resulted in them treating each other with more respect and care. The study was conducted with a very small sample size in a limited timeframe. The authors speculate that this training program has the potential to increase well-being, particularly for those who are most motivated.

The three Post-Positivist mixed methods studies presented in this section illustrate the influence of this paradigm's assumptions on methodological choices. The researchers prioritized the collection of quantitative data based on the ontological assumption that there is a reality that can be measured and the epistemological assumption that researchers' bias can be limited by quantitatively measuring the dependent variables. They adhered to the axiological assumption by following the ethical review requirements of their institution. RCT or quasi-experimental designs allowed them to control for the effect of extraneous variables and determine the effectiveness of interventions. Qualitative data played a supportive role to inform development of interventions, to understand the participants' experiences, and to aid interpretation of the quantitative findings. In the next section, the Constructivist paradigm assumptions are discussed, and examples are used to illustrate its application in research design.

Mixed Methods and the Constructivist Paradigm

The Constructivist paradigm has long been associated with the use of qualitative methods. However, even in its early stages of development, the collection of quantitative data was included as a potential supplemental method (Guba and Lincoln 1989). As Guba and Lincoln pointed out, the decision to prioritize qualitative data collection rests on a set of assumptions. Table 2.2 displays the assumptions associated with the Constructivist paradigm.

Ethically, the Constructivist paradigm calls upon researchers to go beyond the institutional ethical review criteria. Ethics about interactions with members of the studied communities raise issues of whose voice is heard and the quality of rapport built between the researcher and the participants. The Constructivist paradigm's ontological assumption is that "social reality is constructed and that subjective meaning is a critical component of knowledge building" (Hesse-Biber, Rodriguez and Frost 2015: 4). The Constructivist's approach to mixed methods rests on the assumption that "social

TABLE 2.2 Philosophical Assumptions of the Constructivist Paradigm

Axiology: Researchers conduct their studies in compliance with institutional ethical criteria, but they are also cognizant of the need to provide balanced representation of views, give participants the opportunity to have their voices heard, and the need to build rapport with the participants.
Ontology: The assumption is made that reality is multiple and socially constructed.
Epistemology: The assumption is made that researchers and participants need to have an interactive link in order to co-construct the realities; attention is given to the multiplicity of values that influence understandings of realities; findings are co-created by researchers and participants.
Methodology: Qualitative methods are dominant with quantitative methods playing a supportive role. Contextual variables are considered to be very important and need to be included in the interpretation of findings.

reality is subjective, consisting of narratives or meanings constructed/co-constructed by individuals and others within a specific social context" (Hesse-Biber et al. 2015: 4). This stands in sharp contrast to the Post-Positivist's ontological assumption that there is a reality out in the world that can be measured, albeit imperfectly.

The Constructivist researcher chooses methods that support contextual understandings and allows for the influence of the participants' voices to be front and center (Mertens 2020a). Qualitative methods such as participant observation, in-depth interviews, focus groups, and document reviews are used to capture the complexity of the phenomenon. Quantitative measures can be added to a qualitatively driven study framed within the Constructivist paradigm to answer "*a subquestion or set of subquestions that assist in the elaboration or clarification of overall core qualitatively driven research questions(s)*" (Hesse-Biber et al. 2015: 5, italics in the original). A Constructivist chooses methods that align with the Constructivist assumptions about ethics and values, the nature of reality, and knowledge. Hence the choice of in-depth interviews makes sense because there is a need to obtain "deeper and more genuine expressions of beliefs and values that emerge through dialogue [and] foster a more accurate description of views held" (Howe 2004: 54, cited in Hesse-Biber et al. 2015: 6). If the desire is to understand the effect of an intervention, Maxwell (2004) argues that the use of qualitative methods is essential to demonstrating the way that the intervention caused (or failed to cause) the intended effects.

There are many possible reasons to integrate quantitative methods into a qualitatively driven study (Hesse-Biber et al. 2015). For example, a researcher might want to use a quantitative demographic survey to obtain a picture of community members. The survey results could be used as a basis for the selection of a smaller sample that includes salient characteristics for a more in-depth qualitative part of a study. The larger survey might surface smaller groups within the community that might have been overlooked otherwise. If the qualitative sample is chosen to be representative of the larger population, it can contribute to stronger assertions about the transferability of findings (or generalizability in Post-Positivist terms). The comparison of quantitative and qualitative data sets can contribute to a better understanding of the phenomenon or even raise new research questions that could be explored in the future.

Case Studies of Mixed Methods with the Constructivist Paradigm

Mixed Methods Constructivist Case Study #1: Living with Dementia

Harding, Sullivan, Yong, and Crutch (2021) provide an interesting example of a qualitatively dominant mixed methods study that used a case study with focused ethnographic methods and quantitative psychological measures to study people living at home with dementia. They described their study as "a mixed-methods home-based observational study to explore how the challenges in these intersecting environments are navigated in real time and in the social and relational context in which they occur, while also exploring how a variety of data sources might contribute to this understanding" (236). They had two main research questions:

- Which activities are people taking part in and why? (Who instigates this and how? Are they familiar or new activities? Are they predominantly socially or physically engaging, or both? What does the activity provide?)

- How is participation in activities challenged and/or supported? (Who instigates this? Do physical objects help or hinder with this? How?)

(243)

Harding et al. (2021) supported their choice of a qualitative case study because it allows researchers to study complex real-world problems that are contextually dependent and where the many interrelated variables cannot be controlled. Harding's team emphasized the importance of building rapport and trust with the participants through empathetic, deep listening. They explained that focused ethnography is different from classical ethnography in that it does not require prolonged immersion in the field – a constraint often faced in healthcare research. In this approach, the ethnographic questions are more focused, although there is room for revision and addition as the researcher comes to understand the socially constructed meanings of a specific cultural group. The researchers followed the constructivist guidance to critically reflect on their own values and roles by keeping detailed journals while they were in the field. They prioritized the constructivist epistemological assumption by designing the study to capture multiple perspectives and subjective meanings.

The qualitative data were collected during home visits; the researchers did not provide specific information about the number of homes or the duration of the visits (Harding et al. 2021). Video data were collected by a camera that was worn by the person with dementia and so provided an approximation of their view of the world. The video recordings captured interactions between the person with dementia and their primary care giver in their home. This data included informal conversations, how the participants used the space, and their proximity to other people and objects, among other things. The researchers supplemented the video data with field notes that were recorded on time-labeled worksheets so they could coordinate the two sources of data. Harding and colleagues discussed the ethical issues associated with close contact with the participants related to being respectful and building trust. They noted the importance of spending time with people to get to know them and to make them feel comfortable. The elements of importance were empathy, listening, staying in the moment, and being nonjudgmental. They were aware of the sensitive nature of the topic (dementia) and the stress that engendered in their participants and tried to minimize that by seeing them as whole human beings with multiple interests, not simply people with cognitive impairments.

The quantitative portion of Harding et al.'s (2021) study included the use of neuropsychological assessments of cognitive functions, including memory, attention, language, and visual spatial functioning. These instruments are standardized and are designed to objectively assess a person's level of impairment. Other quantitative data were collected from self-reports of memory difficulties, depression, apathy, and the ability to perform daily activities. Physiological data were also collected using accelerometer data to capture a person's level of physical activity and measurement of heart rate in responses to stress or excitement. A graphic depiction of their mixed methods design is provided in Figure 2.2.

During the data analysis phase, the researchers used a visual display of data for each participant to integrate the quantitative

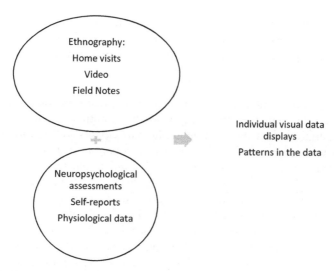

FIGURE 2.2 *Mixed Methods Ethnographic Case Study of the Dementia Experience (Adapted from Harding et al. 2021).*

and qualitative data (Harding et al. 2021). The display was in essence a mixed methods picture of data for each participant. The codes that emerged for each participant were put at the center of the display along with specific quotations from the video and field notes. The quantitative data were displayed around the qualitative data and included age of diagnosis and results of the neuropsychology assessment and the self-report scales. In this way, the researchers could see each participant as a case with unique characteristics. They could then organize the cases with commonalities and differences to identify patterns. They described the advantages of using mixed methods that emerged during the data analysis as follows:

> During the analysis, triangulation of qualitative data sources happened throughout, and triangulation of the mixed-methods data sources occurred toward the end of the analytic process (as recommended) as multiple data sources and the varied interpretations of them were juxtaposed and used to test one another. The quantitative data were used to potentially aid

innovative interpretations of the qualitative data, and this
process in turn illuminated potential ways that qualitative data
could help inform the interpretation of the quantitative.

(247)

One strength of the study was that a fuller picture of the people
with dementia emerged by juxtaposing the quantitative data with
the qualitative data. For example, one participants' self-report of
ability to engage in daily life activities was quantitatively very low.
However, observations indicated that this individual spent several
hours outside clearing leaves by hand in his yard. This participant
said that he wanted to do something physical, especially since he
had had to quit work after his diagnosis. Results like this shifted the
researchers' thinking from focusing on deficits to how people living
with dementia find meaning in their lives. Generally, the advantage
of using mixed methods with this population was summarized as
follows:

> It became clear that contrasting the video and physiological
> data could be useful not only for recontextualizing to clarify
> but also for demonstration and appreciation of the complexity
> of the scenarios we were observing and as a reminder of the
> limitations of any single data source in building a representation
> of something as variable and individual as a person's lived
> experience. Although analyzing these rich and complex moments
> with multiple data sources did not always mean a clear and
> undisputable interpretation could be made, the combination of
> data sources helped toward our understanding of the complexity
> of the everyday environment, the limitations of the data collection
> tools, both individually and together, and the potential scope or
> parameters of the research questions we are able to ask within
> such settings.

(255)

Harding et al. (2021) had many strengths based on the collection
of many types of qualitative data that allowed different versions
of reality to be illuminated. Their integration of the data occurred
when they developed charts for each participant that incorporated
the results of the quantitative data with the qualitative data.
This enabled them to understand the nature of the participants'

experiences and to better interpret their results. They did not use the data to change any intervention strategies – only to describe the nature of the experience.

Mixed Methods Constructivist Case Study #2: Mindfulness Training

Cheek and associates (2015) conducted a qualitatively dominant mixed methods study that was designed to investigate the long-term effects of mindfulness training. The mindfulness training was designed to improve the students' social and emotional well-being. The students were aged nine to eleven years when they participated in mindfulness training in an elementary school in the United States. However, the study took place when the participants were young adults in their late twenties in order to determine the long-term effects of the training. The study was designed to understand "how mindfulness-based programs can be implemented on a daily basis, the settings in which this occurs, and how the programs might be received by the students from their point of view" (754–5). Interestingly, the study was initially conceived as a quantitatively dominant mixed methods study. The design shifted to become a qualitatively dominant design as a result of discussions among the research team members that included experts in qualitative and quantitative methods. Their conversations led them to the conclusion that the idea of measuring the long-term effects using mainly quantitative measures was too narrow because they also wanted to know "participants' perceptions about the effects of the MT curriculum on their lives, including what they could remember about it, how they perceived it had or had not affected their lives, and whether they continue to use what they had learned some 20 years earlier" (756).

Dynamic reflexivity, a hallmark of qualitative methodologies, was an important part of the study (Cheek et al. 2015). It helped the research team understand what they meant by effects; this clarification led to a better understanding of what they wanted to know and why. The quantitative part of the study included a battery of measures that were administered simultaneously with the qualitative data collection. Critical reflection on the types of interviews, who to interview, and the focus of the interviews influenced the qualitative part of the study. The point of integration was at the formulation of the results narrative.

As the researchers continued their critical reflection through dialogue with each other, the qualitative part of the study shifted. Initially, the qualitative researchers planned to use semi-structured interviews to explore what the participants recalled about their mindfulness training, how they perceived the effects, how the effects affected their lives, and whether they continue to use the mindfulness strategies in their current lives (Cheek et al. 2015). However, they began their use of qualitative data through a document review of letters the students wrote at the time of the training to the developer of the mindfulness program. The researchers had access to 188 letters in which the students described their experiences in terms of what happened in the classroom and how they felt about the training. Upon reading a few of the letters, the researchers realized they were a rich source of data and decided to read all of them and code them using accepted qualitative data analysis techniques. The results of this document review led them to change how they would use the interviews. The interviewers still asked about the four areas previously identified, but the researchers decided to conduct interviews with specific letter writers and probe specific areas that had surfaced in the document review. The emergence of new questions and modifications of methods is another hallmark of qualitative methodologies.

The integration of the qualitative and quantitative data is ongoing. At the time the article was published (Cheek et al. 2015), the researchers were exploring ways to integrate the qualitative and quantitative findings. They suggested that they could develop in-depth case studies of the effects of the training on individual students that encompassed the results of the quantitative measures and the qualitative data for specific participants. The study had an emerging design with a very strong qualitative component (as would be expected in the Constructivist paradigm). The quantitative component was secondary; the integration of the two types of data is for the purpose of understanding the effects of the program. As the researchers were working with an intervention that occurred many years before they began their study, they were not able to influence the nature of the training.

Mixed Methods Constructivist Case Study #3: Imagery and Athletes

Kacperski, Ulloa, and Hall (2019) provide a third example of a qualitatively dominant mixed methods study in which they explored how athletes use concrete and abstract imagery in and around competition. They describe their study as a mixed methods research phenomenological study. They presented qualitative and quantitative research questions. Their qualitative questions asked: "How [do] levels of abstraction appear in imagery and *why*, that is, their functionality. The quantitative [questions ask] … *what*, that is, which abstractions levels are used in what way and when, but also allows for clarification through mixed methods integration to find why some athletes of different sports prefer abstract or concrete imagery" (217). In addition, the researchers added a quantitative dimension in the data analysis stage when they created quantitative categories based on the qualitative data.

Data collection was primarily qualitative supplemented by a demographic questionnaire (Kacperski et al. 2019). The participants were university students in Canada who had participated in national-level competitions. The countries of origin were quite diverse with participants from Canada, China, Egypt, India, and Germany. They represented a variety of different sports, including track running, triple jump, discus, golf, table tennis, badminton, judo, and boxing. While the researchers label their study as phenomenological, the qualitative interviews they conducted only averaged twenty-three minutes; the authors recognized this as a limitation in their study. The students were asked about their participation in sport in practice and competition, their use of imagery at various time points (e.g., the day before competition, at the competition, and at the completion of the competition), and the usefulness of the imagery. Following qualitative data analysis strategies, the interviews were transcribed, coded, and organized into higher level themes.

In addition to the quantitative demographic data, the researchers included another strategy for integrating quantitative and qualitative data. They transformed the qualitative data by extracting numerical data based on the use of imagery, type of imagery (concrete, abstract), time levels, type of sport, and reported effectiveness of the imagery.

The researchers were then able to create tables that displayed the frequencies of codes associated with the use of concrete or abstract imagery, when they used the imagery, and its perceived usefulness by type of sport. The integration of the qualitative and quantitative data contributed to a better understanding of the use of imagery by athletes. For example, the qualitative data revealed that athletes used concrete imagery to imagine themselves playing their sport the way they wanted to in the competition; the quantitative analysis revealed that this was the most common use of imagery. The study was not intended to enhance athletes' use of imagery in competition; they only wanted to describe how the athletes used the imagery.

The Constructivist mixed methods studies described in this section illustrate how the assumptions of this paradigm influence methodological choices. The studies reflected the Constructivist ontological assumption that reality is constructed; thus, they employed strategies to build understandings of participants' experiences through interviews, observations, and document reviews. They discussed the importance of building rapport and being respectful of participants; this reflects both the axiological and epistemological Constructivist assumptions. They used traditional Constructivist methodologies such as ethnography and phenomenology; they allowed the research question to evolve throughout the conduct of the study. And they supplemented the qualitative data collection with quantitative data. Integration in qualitatively dominant studies takes different forms; it can be used to describe the nature of experiences and to enhance the researcher's ability to document effects of programs. In the next section, the assumptions of the Pragmatic paradigm are explained and case studies are used to illustrate its application in mixed methods research design.

Mixed Methods and a Pragmatic Paradigm

Teddlie and Tashakkori (2003) suggested that framing mixed methods from a pragmatic lens would overcome concerns that conflicting assumptions found in the Post-Positivist and Constructivist paradigms, which some called the incompatibility problem, would prevent the mixing of methods. The Pragmatic paradigm holds that mixed methods is appropriate because they can be used to answer research questions that require both quantitative and qualitative data (Tashakkori, Johnson, and Teddlie 2021). However, this "what works" interpretation of pragmatism has been criticized as a misrepresentation of the philosophy of pragmatism as it was presented by such scholars as John Dewey, William James, Richard Rorty, and Charles Pierce (Denzin 2012; Hall 2013).

Tashakkori et al. (2021) acknowledge the different kinds of pragmatism and suggest that elements of these different philosophies associated with pragmatism could provide a basis for the choice of using mixed methods. However, they present a more generic framing for the Pragmatic paradigm in the mixed methods community. They describe their philosophical interpretation of pragmatism as follows: "The two major characteristics of pragmatism are (a) the rejection of the dogmatic either-or choice between constructivism and post-positivism (or any other paradigms) and (b) the desire to search for useful answers to research questions of interest to the investigator" (62). The philosophical assumptions of the Pragmatic paradigm are displayed in Table 2.3.

TABLE 2.3 Philosophical Assumptions of the Pragmatic Paradigm

Axiology: The researcher's values guide the selection of the research topic and questions in order to fulfill the purpose of the research study and to make the world a better place (according to Dewey).

Ontology: There is a single reality that can be experienced differently by different individuals.

Epistemology: Relationships are developed in ways the researcher deems appropriate for each study, although researchers should be as objective as possible and knowledge claims should rely on empirical data.

Methodology: Use mixed methods to answer questions that are best answered using those methods.

Adapted from Mertens (2018; 2020a), Plano Clark and Ivankova (2016), and Tashakkori et al. (2021).

Case Studies of the Pragmatic Approach to Mixed Methods

Mixed Methods Pragmatic Case Study #1: Teachers and Stress

This first example of mixed methods research framed by the Pragmatic paradigm was conducted to explore the effect of stressful conditions on teachers (Bogaert, De Martelaer, Deforche, Clarys, and Zinzen 2015). Rather than asking teachers about their needs with regard to changes needed to reduce their stress (as would be done in the Transformative paradigm, discussed in the next section), these researchers focused their study on how teachers could reduce their stress through physical exercise based on the findings of medical research that suggests that physical exercise can lead to reduced feelings of stress (Tang, Leka, and MacLennan 2013). Bogaert and colleagues decided to address the very practical problem of describing the physical activity levels of secondary teachers in Flanders in Belgium, characteristics of less active teachers, barriers to engaging in physical activities, and possibilities for workplace interventions to increase activity.

Bogaert at al. (2015) described their mixed methods design as being framed by the Pragmatic paradigm. They used a parallel mixed methods design, meaning that both quantitative and qualitative data were collected simultaneously (see Figure 2.3). Quantitative data were collected by means of an online version of the International Physical Activity Questionnaire; it yielded data on teachers' physical activity at work and at home, as well as transport-related physical activity and sitting time. Qualitative data were collected through focus groups in order to understand ideas, feelings, and other factors that influenced development and implementation of worksite interventions. The authors reported that they had received ethical approval through their university ethics review committee and the participants had provided informed consent.

Bogaert and colleagues (2015) reported the results of the quantitative survey and the qualitative focus groups separately. The integration of findings from the two approaches occurred in the

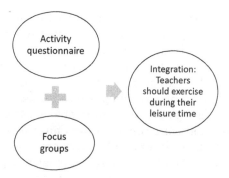

FIGURE 2.3 *A Pragmatic Parallel Mixed Methods Design of Teacher Stress (Adapted from Bogaert et al. 2015).*

discussion portion of their article. The quantitative results indicated that about two-thirds of the teachers reported engaging in over 150 minutes of activity per week. The focus groups reported that worksite interventions were generally not practical because they were already busy during lunch breaks and had responsibilities after work, such as transporting children or groceries. Active transport to and from work was also not practical due to these same constraints. There is no indication that these results were shared with the participating schools or that teachers changed their behaviors based on the findings. The researchers chose the research topic and questions; they did not involve the teachers in the process of developing or implementing the study. The authors used these findings to recommend possible interventions, such as encouraging teachers to be more active in their leisure time. They did not involve the teachers in making recommendations on how to reduce stress.

Mixed Methods Pragmatic Case Study #2: Food Emergencies

A pragmatic approach is illustrated by Shannon, Borron, Kurtz, and Weaver's (2021) use of a mixed methods design to address a food emergency problem in Atlanta, Georgia. The Atlanta Community Food Bank provided a means for surplus food from corporations or individuals to be distributed to people who were experiencing food insecurity in the Atlanta area. The staff at the food bank recognized that simply providing food to people in need was not sufficient to address the underlying reasons for ongoing need, such as low wages, fewer social assistance services due to cut-backs, and high healthcare costs. They wanted to explore how they could provide more holistic services by partnering with other agencies to reduce food insecurity through access to affordable housing and sources of income. The food bank contacted the University of Georgia to ask for their assistance in solving this very practical problem. The researchers framed their work using the pragmatic philosophical paradigm and a culture-centered approach to communication.

> Pragmatism emphasizes the socially embedded nature of knowledge (Feilzer, 2009; Harney et al. 2016), and enrolls diverse social actors to name pressing problems and develop solutions, a process referred to within pragmatism as *inquiry* (Barnes, 2008; Lake, 2017). The epistemological flexibility of pragmatist research—its emphasis on considering the world through different vantage points—makes it well suited for mixed methods research. In our case, pragmatism's emphasis on communities of inquiry was particularly useful as a framework.
>
> (118)

The use of the Pragmatic paradigm is evidenced by their focus on an actionable research problem using a participatory methodological approach because they wanted to highlight those structural factors that contribute to food insecurity. Their intent was not to conduct research that would move directly to collective action (as would be the case in transformative research). Rather, their findings were intended to lead to discussions of policy change that were relevant to the topics uncovered in their study.

The researchers chose to use concept mapping because it is an inherently mixed methods approach (Shannon et al. 2021). It is similar to focus groups in that perspectives are solicited from multiple individuals (qualitative); integration of the data occurs by changing the qualitative data into quantitative data. In concept mapping these qualitative data are then combined using quantitative clustering techniques such as multidimensional scaling and factor analysis to identify shared opinions. In this study the qualitative statements were generated by the use of photo elicitation, i.e., the participants generated images that were used to elicit ideas about where the food bank could provide support for food insecure households. Participants were encouraged to take pictures of the times and places in their lives where they get, transport, prepare, or eat food. "Our project draws out the potential for these two methods to facilitate collective discovery of dynamics shaping household food security and instability, an approach designed to encourage the development of innovative approaches to empowering food pantry clientele" (117).

Shannon et al. (2021) also discussed the practical problems when conducting mixed methods using teams with different experiences and backgrounds. Their team included researchers who were strong in qualitative methods and others who were strong in quantitative methods. Food bank staff were also members of the research team and brought their own personal experiences to the study. Together the research team members worked to be flexible in their employment of epistemological and methodological approaches. The diversity of their team provided the inclusion of research methodological expertise in qualitative and quantitative methods, as well as the practical experiences of the food bank staff.

One strength of the study was that the researchers included agency staff, volunteers, and clients in data collection and interpretation. The use of the photo elicitation and focus group data collection methods allowed different perspectives to emerge. The concept mapping resulted in quantitative representations of the clients' needs and experiences that could be shared with policymakers. The researchers organized an interagency summit to discuss the results and allow service providers with an opportunity to create ideas for modifying service models at their agencies. The combination of the qualitative and quantitative data provided personal stories along with patterns of results; this is a strength of the qualitatively dominant mixed methods approach.

Mixed Methods Pragmatic Case Study #3: Parenting in Single-Child Families

Khadaroo and MacCallum (2021) conducted a third example of a mixed methods study using the Pragmatic paradigm to understand the parenting of adolescents in British single-child families. Their interest in the subject arose from a trend in the UK toward families deciding to have a single child and the associated stereotype that only-children are spoiled and given too much attention by their parents. Their research question was: "How do the parenting styles and practices used in single-child families with adolescent children compare to those in multiple children families?" (3–4). They chose a mixed methods design because they posited that it would provide a more comprehensive understanding of this complex topic. They received ethical approval from their university ethics committee, parents signed informed consents, and adolescents signed assent forms (as they were under the age of consent, their agreement to participate was dependent on their parents' approval and the adolescents' agreement to participate).

Khadaroo and MacCallum (2021) used an "embedded design with a two-phase approach [that] incorporated a qualitative section (semi-structured interviews) that could support the quantitative (online survey) findings" (4). According to Plano Clark and Ivankova (2016), an embedded design is one in which one type of data collection dominates.

> Embedded designs are defined as having an unequal priority in terms of the relative importance of the quantitative and qualitative components for addressing the study's research questions. Researchers choose an embedded approach when their research questions include primary and secondary questions, where one question (e.g., the primary question) calls for a quantitative approach and the other question (e.g., the secondary question) calls for a qualitative approach. Contrasted with the primary research questions, the secondary questions are described as having lesser priority and addressing different (but related) questions that aim to enhance the implementation or interpretation of the larger design. In relation to the research questions, the embedded method has less priority, is located within and constrained by the larger design, and its role within the study has been described as supplementary, subservient, and supportive.
>
> (Plano Clark et al. 2013: 223)

In Khadaroo and MacCallum's (2021) study, the quantitative data part of the study was dominant; the qualitative portion played a supplemental role. Quantitative data were collected using standardized instruments that were administered online. Parents completed the Parenting Styles and Dimensions Questionnaire-Short Version (Robinson et al. 2001) to identify their parenting styles and the Parents of Adolescents Separation Anxiety Scale (Hock et al. 2001) to assess their feelings of anxiety when separated from their children. Adolescents completed two standardized instruments as well: the Parental Authority Questionnaire (Buri 1991) to assess their views on their parents' parenting styles and the Child-Parent Relationship Test (Titze and Lehmkuhl 2010) to examine their relationship to each parent (mother/father). Qualitative data were collected through semi-structured interviews to probe the participants' perceptions of parenting experiences and practices.

The survey data were analyzed using factor analysis and regression analysis (Khadaroo and MacCallum 2021). Factor scores were calculated and compared for single and multiple-children families; no statistically significant results were found, with the exception that single-child adolescents reported more negative parenting with their fathers. Regression analysis was used to test the predictors of positive parenting; no significant differences were found between the two family types. Some differences did emerge from the qualitative data. For example, children in multiple-children homes reported that their parents were more authoritative more frequently than did only-children. Only-children also reported that they spent more time with their parents than did non-single-child families. Integration of the findings occurred at the discussion stage of the study and helped to explain the findings. For example the lack of differences on the questionnaire results challenges the stereotype that single children are spoiled. Parents from both types of families reported that they prioritized their child's needs over their own, respected their autonomy, and gave them freedom of choice, within limits. Single children were more likely to describe their parents as being over-protective; however, this was couched in their realization that they spent more time with their parents and that they had a positive relationship. The researchers described the advantage of using mixed methods as follows: "The mixed-method approach meant that the *lived* parenting experiences and the adolescents' experience of being parented in single-child families were more intricately revealed from family interviews than family surveys" (19).

Two strengths of this study are that they collected data to answer the research questions in an expedient manner and the integration of the quantitative and qualitative data at the interpretation stage. This allowed more informed conclusions to be drawn. The researchers did not involve families in the development of the research questions or the strategies for data collection. No recommendations emerged from the study for parenting practices.

Mixed Methods Pragmatic Case Study #4: Big Data and Health Services

Big data is appearing more and more in the research literature as a potential treasure trove, providing opportunities for developing innovative approaches, as well as presenting new challenges. Holtrop, Potworowski, Green, and Fetters (2019) provide a fourth example of a pragmatically framed study using big data in a mixed methods study that explored the provision of primary care for persons with chronic health conditions in the United States. They described the practical problem that they wanted to address in their research as follows: "The goals in health services research are to improve patient outcomes while increasing efficiency and managing the unsustainable growth in cost, a particularly compelling challenge in the United States, but increasingly a problem in many rapidly aging countries in Europe and Asia" (87). They supported their choice of a pragmatic approach as one that provided health insurers and administrators with results in a quicker timeframe than would be possible with other approaches. The insurers and administrators want to have findings delivered in a timely fashion from research that does not compromise their ability to continue with their provision of services.

Holtrop et al. (2019) used a convergent mixed methods design, meaning that quantitative and qualitative data were collected simultaneously as separate research tracks, with integration at the end of the study. "The purpose of a convergent design is to obtain different but complementary data on the same topic with the intent to bring together the strengths of both quantitative and qualitative methods" (92). The purpose of the study was to use "mixed methods to compare the effectiveness of two models of care management delivery: health plan delivered care management (health plan) versus provider-delivered care management (provider-delivered)" (90). Health plan management is a for-profit program purchased by employers to benefit their employees. The health plan creates algorithms to identify patients with chronic diseases who might benefit from participating in a disease management program. In provider-delivered plans, physicians designed the care management plans for their own organizations. The variables of interest included determining the success of each type of program and identifying the factors that influenced the success of the two types of care management programs.

The quantitative portion of the study was dominant and consisted of access to data from over 12,000 physicians and patients (big data) that was available from existing databases (Holtrop et al. 2019). The data had been collected as part of the medical care programs and consisted of physician monthly reports, medical records, and insurance claims data. The outcomes of interest included measures of the extent of patient engagement (how much did patients participate in the program), clinical values such as blood pressure or weight, and health care claims that resulted in costs to the insurance company. In addition, a small number (51) of leaders of the care organizations, physicians, and patients completed a quantitative survey. The survey was designed to gather data on the health care practices and the context in which those services were provided. The results of the quantitative analysis of the big data indicated that provider-delivered plans were more effective in patient engagement and cost savings; no significant differences were found on clinical outcomes.

Qualitative data were collected by interviewing five leaders of provider-delivered organizations, seventy care providers, and six health plan leaders (Holtrop et al. 2019). The interviews asked about the process of care delivery, the characteristics of participants, and how the programs were implemented. In addition, two researchers conducted observations at twenty-five care delivery sites. The qualitative data were analyzed using standard coding procedures that yielded themes that were considered to represent the components of care management that were routinely used. These components were then put into a quantitative form that allowed the researchers to rate provider-delivered plans on their implementation of these components on a three-point scale (high, medium, and low). This process is a form of integration of quantitative and qualitative data and is known as "quantitizing" qualitative data. Using these transformed quantitative data, the researchers were able to identify program features that were associated with different outcomes.

In order to complete this complex study, a large research team was used to encompass the diverse skill sets needed in research methods and health care (Holtrop et al. 2019). Representatives from two medical schools, a research institution, health insurers, epidemiologists, and statisticians were part of the team. The team functioning was aided by having previous agreements on the use of the data and about everyone being eligible for authorship on publications.

These four Pragmatic mixed methods studies illustrate the application of this paradigm to research problems of a very practical nature. The researchers wanted to know about the level of physical activity of teachers, how partnerships might improve food delivery to those in need, whether parents of single-child families spoiled their children, and how to improve health care for people with chronic conditions. The designs focused on the collection of data to answer specific research questions. There was little community involvement in the development of the research questions or strategies or in the interpretation of the data. The use of the data for transformative purposes was limited; this contrasts with the Transformative approach to mixed methods discussed in the next section.

Mixed Methods and the Transformative Paradigm

The Transformative paradigm emerged in response to the voices of members of marginalized and vulnerable communities who argued that research as traditionally conducted misrepresented them, left them worse off, or dealing with interventions that did not adequately meet their needs (McBride, Casillas, and LoPiccolo 2020; Mertens 2020a). As the world faces dramatic challenges, such as the climate crisis, a global pandemic, and an increasing gap between rich and poor with the concomitant consequences of these inequities, researchers can ask themselves these questions: How does my research sustain an oppressive status quo? And a parallel question: How can I structure my research so that it leads to a more just world? Critical reflection on answers to these questions can be guided by the assumptions of the Transformative paradigm (see Table 2.4).

The transformative axiological assumption provides the framing for the other assumptions in this paradigm (Mertens 2020a). If ethics in research is considered to be based on addressing discrimination and an oppressive status quo, then the research needs to be responsive to the diversity in cultures within the context of the study. The criteria for ethical review that are commonly used in institutions are useful and warrant attention, but according to members of vulnerable and marginalized communities, the criteria have not been sufficient to protect them from the negative effects of research or to improve conditions in their communities. The concept of ethics in the Transformative paradigm is expanded to include cultural responsiveness, addressing inequities, giving back

TABLE 2.4 Philosophical Assumptions of the Transformative Paradigm

Axiology: Research needs to be structured to address issues of discrimination and oppression and to lead to increased social, economic, and environmental justice.
Ontology: Realities are recognized as coming from different positionalities; some of these versions of reality lead to sustained oppression; others have the potential to lead to increased justice.
Epistemology: Relationships need to be formed with the full range of people impacted by the research (stakeholders) with particular attention to those who have traditionally been excluded from decision-making. Relationships need to be responsive to culture and context and consciously address issues of power inequities. Knowledge gained by lived experience is valued and integrated into the research process and the use of the findings.
Methodology: Mixed methods are generally needed in order to capture the complexity of the context, understand the need for action, and develop interventions that are culturally responsive and supportive of increased justice.
Adapted from Mertens (2020a; 2018) and Mertens and Wilson (2019)

to the communities (reciprocity), and providing a foundation for transformative change (Mertens and Catsambas 2022). Mixed methods can be useful to identify the diversity within the community that need to be included in order to be responsive to the full range of stakeholders and to contribute to increased justice. This means that methodologically, the researcher needs to include time in the design of the research to collect contextual data and to form culturally respectful relationships that demonstrate that they value the dignity and worth of community members.

Reciprocity is another dimension of the transformative ethical assumption that has ontological, epistemological, and methodological implications (Mertens 2020a). If reciprocity is defined in terms of increased justice and contributing to transformative change, then researchers need to include members of the marginalized and vulnerable communities that are structured to value their knowledge and experience. Inclusion of members of marginalized and vulnerable communities and valuing their knowledge and experience can result in making visible the versions of reality that sustain oppression and lead to increased understandings of what is needed to have transformative and just changes. This allows for the research to be conducted in line with the transformative ontological assumption. One strategy that can be used in transformative research is to build capacities in communities without experience in conducting and using research. In order to support needed changes, the researcher can structure the research to include a coalition of stakeholders that can inform the research design and provide for sustainability in the communities once the study is ended (Wolfe, Price and Brown 2020).

Methodologically, transformative studies can incorporate many different approaches; however, these approaches need to be framed using a transformative lens. This means that researchers do not assume that they know exactly who needs to be included and how to include them until they begin to collect data during a phase of relationship building. This phase can overlap with contextual analysis where data are collected about the history, politics, legislation, economic conditions, education, health, and types of social services that are relevant in the context. Data collected during the relationship building and contextual analysis phases can lead to the development of interventions that are viewed as valuable and culturally responsive. Data can then be collected on the implementation and effects of the intervention on a pilot basis. If the community is in agreement, then the intervention could be implemented on a larger scale. Throughout the study, the data that are collected are used in ways that support transformations in the research process itself, the community, and the larger context.

Case Studies of the Transformative Approach to Mixed Methods

Transformative Mixed Methods Case Study #1: Health Care for Bi/gay Men and Trans-Women

Miller (2020) provides an example of a transformative mixed methods study in her study on access to and quality of culturally responsive health care for gay and bisexual men and trans-women in Cameroon, a country in which members of these sexual minority groups face discrimination, stigma, and violence. The name of the research study, the Advocacy and other Community Tactics Project (ACT), provides insights into the overtly transformative intent of the research. The study was conducted by an external researcher and a collaborative that included a lead activist agency, a watchdogging expert, and nine collaborating identity groups. At first glance, the data collection methods appear to be somewhat traditional: "Evaluation site visits incorporated observations, interviews, and focus groups, and review of documents" (1). The transformative lens is seen by the advocacy stance taken by the collaborative on behalf of the oppressed groups, ensuring grass-roots representation, providing a safe and supportive environment, focusing on justice, and consciously addressing power issues to form a basis for transformative action. The collaboration guided decisions about data collection by gay/bi men and trans-women and provided a mechanism for sustainability. The transformative mixed methods design is displayed in Figure 2.4.

A contextual analysis in Miller's (2020) study revealed that legislation exists in this country that stipulates that same-sex sexual relations are punishable by prison time and even death. Miller documented the incidence of homophobic and transphobic violence

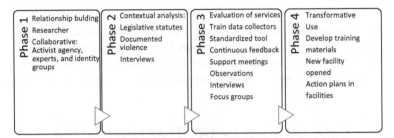

FIGURE 2.4 *Transformative Mixed Methods Design to Improve Health Services for Gay/Bi-Sexual Men and Trans-Women (Adapted from Miller 2020).*

in the country through the use of extant data and interviews with activists. The data on the quality of services were collected by local data collectors who were chosen by the identity organizations to attend training sessions on what to do when visiting health service agencies. An important strength of this study is that data collection involved the use of a standardized tool that was developed in conjunction with members of the bi/gay men and trans-women communities to ensure that it reflected indicators of importance to their community.

As the data collection progressed, the local data collectors reported that they were feeling very stressed and they needed better training on how to safely interact in what was sometimes a very hostile environment, more funding to pay for transportation and medical fees, and more social support (Miller 2020). The advocacy organization responded to their concerns by training the data collectors on how to manage situations in which they experienced discrimination in a nonprovocative manner. Local data collectors were invited to attend support meetings so they could complete their work while they were dealing with the stress of the fieldwork, and they were provided funds for transportation and medical fees.

The quantitative and qualitative data were integrated throughout the study; the contextual information was used to guide the development of the quantitative data instrument (Miller 2020). The combination of the quantitative data from the standardized instrument and the qualitative data from interviews with participants provided a basis for changes in strategies during the study as well as for sharing the results with the full range of stakeholders. The use of the data for transformative purposes went beyond modifications of the methods to being supportive of the data collectors as human beings. The findings were also used to develop training materials for use with healthcare workers and district directors. Transformative changes were seen in the development of action plans by the facilities and districts in which they committed to ongoing training to reduce discriminatory practices, formed a WhatsApp group for district directors to stay informed as issues arose, and established a healthcare services site at one of the identity organizations. In addition, four of the nine identity organizations contributed to the sustainability of the project by training additional people to collect data. The project was focused on a transformation of the healthcare services for this population, and evidence from both quantitative and qualitative data support positive changes were made. A larger transformation is still needed at the legislative level to decriminalize same-sex relations.

Transformative Mixed Methods Case Study #2: School Disparities

In the second transformative mixed methods case study, Garnett, Smith, Kervick, Ballysingh, Moore, and Gonell (2019) illustrate this approach in their investigation of how to improve the educational experiences and outcomes of marginalized and vulnerable youth, given the well-documented school disparities in the United States. They chose a transformative mixed methods approach because it "offers a methodological orientation to legitimize, illuminate, and prioritize perspectives from marginalized youth that may be undervalued, decontextualized, and oversimplified in traditional quantitative and qualitative research methodologies" (2). School reforms in the United States have traditionally been conceptualized and implemented by adults. The historical legacy is that disparities persist in terms of academic achievement, school engagement, and access to supportive behavioral practices. The disparities are manifest on a number of dimensions of diversity, including race/ethnicity, ability, gender, sexual identity, and language. The researchers explicitly describe their role as supporting transformative change in pursuit of school equity to improve "school climate, flatten systematized power hierarchies, and to address entrenched white supremacy in exclusionary discipline" (3).

Garnett and colleagues (2019) conducted their research in a small city in Vermont, a state in the northeastern part of the United States. This school has a diverse population, including a large population of students from recently arrived refugee families; many are English Learners with over forty home languages. This shift in demographics has made visible the White supremacy and ableist legacy of this community that reinforces the superiority of Whiteness and being able bodied, and subjugates Black and Brown students and those with disabilities. The authors argue that White supremacy and ableism are manifest in the zero tolerance exclusionary discipline policies that disproportionately affect racial/ethnic minorities and children with disabilities, feeding a school-to-prison pipeline. Students are suspended at a higher rate if they are from Black or Brown families or have emotional or behavioral disabilities. The result is more frequent involvement with the juvenile justice system for those students who are excluded from school.

The research began at the request of a school district that approached the university to investigate how they could reduce the disparities that resulted from exclusionary discipline procedures (Garnett et al. 2019). The school district had identified an intervention, called restorative practices, that they felt would be a vehicle for reducing suspensions and improving school climate. The university faculty and the school district formed a multi-year partnership that specified the use of a transformative mixed methods action research project and that incorporated Youth Participatory Action Research (YPAR) strategies. In addition to building relationships between the university and school staff, the researchers faced the challenge of building trusting relationships with the students. They asked themselves this difficult question: "How do we as academics in various positions of power and privilege establish trusting relationships with youth to de-colonize the traditional research and scholarship process so that the research topic, question and identification of the problem/asset is truly youth driven?" (Winn and Winn 2016, cited in Garnett et al. 2019: 8).

Part of the research process was dedicated to building trusting relationships with the youth that elevated their voices, flattened the traditional power structure, and changing the curriculum based on student voices. They used multiple strategies in building these relationships:

> These goals were eventually accomplished through a variety of experiential learning activities, vocabulary exercises, and story-telling, all centred on key concepts of critical theory. As a result, by the fourth week of our middle school YPAR project, students were comfortably debating the validity of results from preliminary survey data about perceived gender, religious, and racial discrimination in their school. The flattening of the classroom power structure became evident when students began communicating with adult facilitators several concerns they felt about the ongoing work.
>
> (Garnett et al. 2019: 9)

Evidence of the shift in power relations was documented in the qualitative data when one Black female student learned that the research questions would be decided by the adult facilitators. This resulted in a consciousness raising experience for the adults when they realized that they had violated the principles of YPAR by employing their traditional power to determine the research questions. The questions were revised based on student input so that they were more explicitly focused on accounting for injustices against marginalized groups and discrimination in the school.

Concurrent with the relationship building phase, the researchers and youth conducted a contextual analysis based on extant databases and a preliminary survey that revealed the extent to which there had been an increase in multi-ethnic, multi-lingual families of color in the school district and the disproportionality of suspensions and exclusions from school for these students. Qualitative data were collected through ongoing interactions and opportunities to provide interpretive meaning to the survey data. The integration of the quantitative and qualitative data influenced the development of the data collection instrument and strategies. In line with YPAR and the Transformative paradigm, the restorative practices curriculum was significantly modified to reflect their concerns. This study is ongoing, but the authors raise important questions that are reflective of the application of the transformative mixed methods lens in research, such as:

- How is the critical consciousness of youth used to drive the understanding of the problem and to inform the revision of the intervention, data collection, and analysis?

- How are race and intersections of other forms of oppression centered in the study?

- How are multiple perspectives, multiple methods, and multiple stakeholders integrated to understand the complexities of the restorative practice while explicitly challenging the structural systems of power and privilege?

- "How can we prioritize, elevate and advocate for the narratives of students of colour that may diverge or conflict with established assumptions and quantitatively supported beliefs of 'reality' and 'truth' structured by the current education and disciplinary systems reinforced by traditional models of research?"

(Garnett et al. 2019: 9)

Transformative changes are evident through the use of mixed methods in the initial stages of the Garnett et al. (2019) study. Trusting relationships were built through respectfully responding to the youths' concerns. The young people demonstrated their agency by challenging assumptions of the researchers and the school staff. The curriculum was redesigned to incorporate their concerns. The results of preliminary data collections were interpreted through the eyes of the youth. The final effects of the intervention are not yet available, but the researchers express intent to continue the transformative journey; the students will most likely hold them to it.

Transformative Mixed Methods Case Study #3: Environmental Justice

A third example of a transformative mixed methods includes the use of action research (AR) strategies, building coalitions to inform the process and support sustainability, and a transformative goal of increased environmental justice through effective public deliberations in India (Menon and Hartz-Karp 2020). "The urban problem to be addressed was the lack of intentional street design to meet current needs in a city with high private transport usage, inadequate road safety and streets used as public spaces with multiple, often conflicting social and economic activities" (2). The research team was led by staff from the nonprofit Centre for Environmental Education. Four volunteers from the community and representatives of three local advocacy organizations made up the rest of the team. The structure of the team was very deliberate and based on the assumption that forming "coalitions, civil society organizations could influence the formalization of deep democratic structures and processes which led to further focused conversations on developing such a coalition (or movement)" (8). Thus, the study was designed to be inclusive of diverse voices from the community, building capacity, and supporting sustainable transformative change.

Following the initial development of the team in Menon and Hartz-Karp's (2020) study, they conducted a literature review about the nature of community-based participation in different countries and contexts as a means of gaining understanding of a wide knowledge base on this topic. The team then conducted in-depth qualitative interviews with experts in political science, adult education in the urban setting, rural community-health movements, slum housing, ecological justice, and government bureaucracy. These interviews were part of the contextual analysis that they conducted in order to obtain insight into the socio-political context, current participatory efforts, and strategies for public engagement. The results highlighted the need for equitable and inclusive processes that challenge existing power structures, provide guidance for overcoming barriers, and the critical need to transform urban participation in this region in India. "The inclusion of interviews of expert peers as part of the mixed methods approach complemented the AR and improved its transformative capacity by providing deep context-related insights including practical advice for the conduct of the AR step, and by strengthening the research team's conviction about the value of the research and their commitment to remain actively involved" (8).

Thus results of this qualitative phase of data collection informed the development of a quantitative survey that was conducted in the streets to ascertain how people viewed the current status of civic governance, how they participated in governance, and their interest in and ability to participate in governance decisions (Menon and

Hartz-Karp 2020). Sampling was purposive and designed to be inclusive of thirty different localities across the city that represented residential and commercial areas, as well as a mix of economically well-off and poorer neighborhoods. This survey was administered early in the study to obtain a baseline and then again three years later. The results indicated a gap between what was happening and what was viewed as desirable. Citizens said their experience with governance was mainly being told what policy decisions were made, rather than having active participation in decision-making. The results of the quantitative portion of the study were used for two purposes: first to add questions to the next survey to gain a better understanding of strategies to improve citizen participation in public decision-making, and to clarify the aims of the Action Research phase of the study. "It became clear that the transformation the AR should aim to achieve was high quality, inclusive public deliberations that arrived at a tangible outcome which had the potential to influence the decision-making of the elected and municipal officials" (10). Thus the quantitative and qualitative data were integrated and informed the next stages of the research.

The Action Research phase involved building the capacity of a team of facilitators to conduct public deliberations through an inquiry-based learning experience focused on how to support community participation in an equitable manner. These facilitators then conducted collaborative inquiries with government staff, elected representatives, and resident groups. The inquiry groups were complemented by meetings held with other community groups; the data from these group meetings were used to design the next phase of Action Research. The topic of street improvement was selected based on the expressed needs of the community; the researchers approached the government office responsible for street design and asked for an opportunity for structured deliberations to address the issue. They engaged with a neutral third party, a local NGO with an interest in participatory governance, to manage the process. "The goal was implementing a fair, inclusive deliberation process about street design and mobility planning" (13).

Research processes sometimes appear smooth and seamless when published in journals; however, in the real world, things do not always go as planned. This was true in the Menon and Hartz-Karp (2020) study; the government initially agreed to the structured deliberations but subsequently withdrew its support for this process. The researchers decided to go ahead with the plan to have structured deliberations and shifted the topic from the specific street design focus to the development of a citizen's manifesto on street design. The research team engaged public policy Master's students to collect data from street users, shopkeepers, street vendors, waste collectors, residents, senior citizens, community leaders, and political leaders. Their work revealed a plethora of positions within the community that resulted in conflicts between residents and shopkeepers. The splintering of community voices resulted in the voices of the powerful being the ones that influenced government decisions. The researchers and the NGO invited a wide array of people to participate in a meeting to answer this question: "How do we the people representing all those who live and work on or nearby our streets and travel through them, want our streets to be used, designed, developed and maintained to make our streets places that are productive, safe to enhance the wellbeing for ALL in our community?" (14). The researchers used a quantitative rating system to measure the satisfaction with the representatives, quality of the deliberations, and the opportunities to express their own views and to hear the views of others. Qualitative data were collected via observation by social sector professionals. These data were integrated to guide the interpretation of the results.

Menon and Hartz-Karp (2020) reported that the public deliberations revealed ideas and priorities for street design that would increase environmental health and make the streets safer, such as increasing green cover, decreasing cement, retaining a sense of culture and place, reduction of vehicle congestion, improvement of footpaths and public transport, and increasing safety for women. The results were shared with local authorities who said they would give consideration to these concerns. However, the researchers did not stop there. They shared the results with civic advocacy groups who then took up the cause of including citizen voices in government decision-making. Public officials acknowledged the importance of citizen engagement in street design and subsequently appointed a public relations team, set up an interactive website for citizen engagement, and stated that all stakeholders' views would be taken into consideration. The government officials did follow up by organizing community members over a period of time to update the public on the project. The process of developing inclusive coalitions is not a one-off strategy for success. The coalitions need to continue to be part of the deliberative process even after the research study ends.

Transformative Mixed Methods Case Study #4: Spinal Cord Injuries

Martin Sullivan and team of researchers (2014) in New Zealand provide a fourth example of a transformative mixed methods that focused on improving the engagement of people with spinal cord injuries in research that affects them. They consciously applied a transformative lens to their work in order to address these questions: "Can mixed methods engage appropriately with different members of disability communities, providers, and policy makers; can mixed methods include reciprocity of design to leave the (researched) community better off than prior to the study; and can mixed methods take into account the expertise, knowledge, and strengths of the community for authentic engagement between researchers and the community?" (235). The researchers saw the Transformative paradigm as a useful framework to expand the "nothing about us without us" maxim of the disability community which held that the research in the disability community needed to be conducted by people from that community. They wanted to design a study in which the lead researcher (Sullivan) has a spinal cord injury and other members of the research team would include both persons with spinal cord injuries and those without such injuries.

The team they built included representatives from the two spinal units at hospitals in New Zealand and representatives of consumer groups at the spinal units (Sullivan et al. 2014). They made the explicit decision to use the first phase of their study to recruit and build the skills of members of spinal cord community so they would be equipped to work as co-researchers, not just advisors. The training focused on teaching recruitment strategies and interview techniques. Data collection was described as follows:

It involved three highly structured quantitative interviews done at 4, 12, and 24 months postinjury and two face-to-face qualitative interviews at 6- and 18-month intervals post discharge. The quantitative interviews focused on what was actually happening at the personal, social, and economic levels in the lives of this cohort. The qualitative component focused on the meanings they attributed to these phenomena and how these meanings shaped life chances, life choices, and subjectivity.

(238)

The researchers were deliberately inclusive of Māori who had experienced spinal cord injury and consulted with a Māori healthcare provider who worked with this population.

The transformative effects of the Sullivan et al. (2014) study are most visible in the opportunities provided to members of the spinal cord injuries to build their capacity to engage in the research process. The study had a very high retention rate over the two years; participants said they liked being interviewed by another person with a spinal cord injury. The construction of the mixed team of people with disabilities and without disabilities demonstrates how the voices of those who are traditionally less powerful can be included in ways that level the playing field. The researchers also communicated with policymakers who have indicated an interest in revising policies to make the spinal cord injury supports more equitable.

The four transformative mixed methods studies in this section illustrate the effect of using a transformative lens to frame decisions about methodology. The studies began with building inclusive relationships with a broad range of stakeholders that addressed traditionally inequitable power structures. The issues of discrimination and a legacy of colonialism were directly addressed and strategies were employed to keep these issues centered throughout the research. The researchers also did not begin their studies with the assumption that they knew what the problem was and what the solution should be. They integrated contextual data into their process in order to reach better understandings of how to proceed with research that the community viewed as valuable. The mixed methods included collection of quantitative and qualitative data by methods that were informed by community members. The intent of contributing to transformative change was very consciously addressed. In the next section, the assumptions of an Indigenous paradigm for mixed methods research are discussed and illustrated by case studies that used this framework.

Mixed Methods and an Indigenous Paradigm

Academic research methodologies have largely been grounded in the culture, history, and philosophies of the Euro-Western literature, while ignoring or denigrating the culture, history, and philosophies of Indigenous communities (Chilisa 2020). Indigenous people feel a spiritual connection to the place and people who shape their world; they know how knowledge is created; and they have cultural protocols for respectful engagement with each other, the environment, and the cosmos (Chouinard and Cram 2020). An important aspect of the Indigenous paradigm is its focus on decolonization, not only of its people, but also of the research methodologies used in their communities. This issue is prioritized because of the negative effects of colonization, such as "disease, warfare, an alien and aggressive religion, family disintegration, and the stealing of land" (Chouinard and Cram 2020: 40). The philosophical assumptions of the Indigenous paradigm are displayed in Table 2.5.

The Indigenous axiological assumption reflects the core values that are integral to Indigenous cultures, including prioritizing relationships that manifest "belongingness, togetherness, interdependence, relationships, collectiveness, love and harmony" (Chilisa and Mertens 2021: 247). The methodological implications of the axiological assumption of relationality include valuing community strengths and building relationships that prioritize the knowledge that Indigenous communities bring to informing the purpose, questions, methodologies, data collection strategies, reporting, and dissemination of the research. Epistemologically, this means that the knowledge of the community is sought out to inform understandings of their needs and to develop interventions that are culturally responsive. The Indigenous ontological assumption holds that Indigenous people understand the nature of their own problems and pathways to solutions. Thus, methodologies are needed that are able to make these realities visible so that the focus of research reflects the priorities of the Indigenous community.

Indigenous researchers are responsible for providing reciprocity to community members by supporting increased social, economic, and environmental justice, resisting colonizing forces that silence their communities, and contributing to the health and welfare of their communities (Chilisa and Mertens 2020). These axiological

TABLE 2.5 Philosophical Assumptions of the Indigenous Paradigm

Axiology: The principles of ethics include relationality, responsibility, respect, reverence, reciprocity, reflexivity, responsiveness, and decolonization. Research needs to consider the sustainability of a healthy environment. All things, human and otherwise, share an interconnectedness with a spiritual bond. Research should be conducted with the goals of addressing inequities and discrimination, contributing to social justice, and insuring equitable distribution of rewards.

Ontology: There are multiple constructed realities grounded in material, social, and spiritual contexts and marked by the interconnectedness of the living and non-living and acknowledging relational existence.

Epistemology: Indigenous epistemology sees knowledge as subjective, objective, relational, and inclusive of spiritualty and vision. Indigenization of knowledge is a central aspect and the community plays an essential role. Relationships are everything. There is a need to resist colonial/Western domination.

Methodology: A transformative participatory lens is used to mix Indigenous qualitative and quantitative methods with Western quantitative and qualitative methods.

Adapted from Chilisa (2020) and Chilisa and Mertens (2021).

assumptions overlap somewhat with those of the Transformative paradigm; however, the Indigenous paradigm's focus on reverence, spirituality and values placed on sacred sites and spiritual practices are uniquely associated with this paradigm. Knowledge is not viewed as simply an objective phenomenon that can be measured quantitatively; rather, knowledge is imbued with the sense of spiritual connection and is built through an understanding of history and cultural connections.

The overlap between the Transformative and Indigenous paradigms is not forced; the Indigenous paradigm is viewed as having porous boundaries (Chilisa and Mertens 2020). Discussions of the benefits of putting the Transformative and Indigenous Paradigms in conversation with each other illuminate the common interest in addressing the needs of communities who experience discrimination and oppression (Cram and Mertens 2015; Mertens and Cram 2016). The added value of putting these paradigms together is visible in the raising of different issues through each lens. For example, the Transformative paradigm is viewed as an inclusive umbrella for groups that experience discrimination, thus raising the issue of intersectionality in Indigenous communities. Indigenous communities raise issues of culture that are integral to transformation in their communities, such as spirituality, land sovereignty, and decolonization. The Indigenous paradigm can be combined with other paradigms as well; this is discussed in the next section on case studies of Indigenous mixed methods studies.

Case Studies of the Indigenous Approach to Mixed Methods

Indigenous Mixed Methods Case Study #1: Economic and Educational Benefits in South Africa

Research conducted with farmers in South Africa provides the first example of an Indigenous mixed methods study that had a transformative intent (Arko-Achemfuor, Romm and Serolong 2019; McIntyre-Mills, Karel, Arko-Achemfuor, Romm, and Serolong 2019). The idea for the research came from Lesego Serolong, who is Indigenous to the North West Province in South Africa. She attended her early schooling in the region and went on to obtain advanced degrees in economics. She returned to South Africa with the intention of addressing unemployment, poverty, and malnutrition through helping farmers become more self-reliant, valuing their Indigenous knowledge, and protecting the environment. To this end, she founded Bokamoso Impact Investments as a mechanism developing agriculture and entrepreneurship through innovation and education. The Indigenous mixed methods design is displayed in Figure 2.5.

Lesogo conducted a year of contextual analysis that included collection of quantitative and qualitative data (Arko-Achemfuor et al. 2019). The quantitative data were collected from extant databases about unemployment rates, literacy levels, climate conditions, and economic levels. The qualitative data were collected through observations, interviews, and community meetings. She

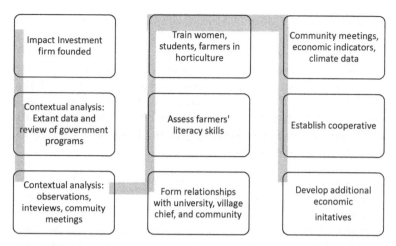

FIGURE 2.5 *Indigenous Mixed Methods Design for South African Farmers (Adapted from Arko-Achemfuor et al. 2019).*

described the process and outcomes of the contextual analysis as follows: "After a year of research in remote Manyeledi and Tseoge villages in the North-West Province—which included an open forum, via town hall meetings to discuss problems existing in the community and possible viable solutions—agriculture and entrepreneurship emerged as a multi-dimensional and holistic solution" (Arko-Achemfuor et al. 2019: 7). Her analysis of government programs and policies revealed that "these interventions give very little practical remedies to the stumbling blocks impeding emerging farmers from accessing the market" (7). Historical analysis revealed that farmers in the region had often been promised life-changing interventions by government, NGOs, and foundations, only to be disappointed.

The contextual analysis led Serolong to approach Arko-Achemfuor who taught at the University of South Africa's (UNISA) Adult Education and Youth Development department to ask if he would teach basic literacy and numeracy skills to farmers in Manyeledi (Arko-Achemfuor et al. 2019). The project reflected a more participatory action focus when Arko-Achemfuor invited Norma Romm, a researcher from South Africa who advocates for Indigenous transformative research; Joyce Karel, a colleague at UNISA's Department of Adult Education and Youth Development;

and Janet McIntyre, a South African with an academic position with Flinders University in Australia, to join the team. The researchers then developed a wider network by inclusion of the village chief, his counsellors, and the farmers, a process made easier because the community already had a tradition of community meetings with the chief. Thus, from the beginning, Indigenous knowledge was valued and existing relationships were strengthened to support the goals of the project. This is in keeping with the Indigenous paradigm's epistemological assumption:

> This way of working together is in keeping with certain Indigenous authors' promulgation of what is called an Indigenous research paradigm, which respects that 'knowing' in Indigenous settings is relational and takes place in communities as people interact with each other in relation to felt challenges. This epistemology (and attendant ethic) has been propounded by Indigenous scholars across the globe (e.g., Arko-Achemfuor and Dzansi 2015 ...) (Arko-Achemfuor et al. 2019: 2).

The research was undertaken with a conscious inclusion of the Indigenous ethical values of respect, appreciation, resilience, and spirituality.

The interventions evolved based on the collection of data in the earlier stages (McIntyre et al. 2019) and integration of new data as it was collected. For example, the intent of Bokamoso Impact Investments was to improve agriculture in sustainable ways based on Indigenous knowledge. However, before the skills of entrepreneurship and marketing could be taught, the data indicated that farmers needed to increase their basic literacy and numeracy skills. Twenty-five farmers, about half male and half female, successfully completed Level 1 of the basic literacy and numeracy classes; the results were measured using quantitative measures set by the Adult Basic Education Training Level program. Once the farmers passed Level 1, they were enrolled in a basic horticulture program. The transformative lens supported consciousness about inclusion of women in the program, in keeping with the intersectionality of Indigenous status and gender. Another intervention was an after-school program to nurture literacy and numeracy skills of children up to age twelve and to help them with their homework. One evolution of the after-school program came from the observation that children needed after-school meals in order to be able to concentrate on their studies. This data was used to put in place the purchase and delivery of food for the children.

The interventions regarding agricultural development also evolved as the level of literacy warranted additional training in production of vegetables on a commercial scale, marketing, and sustainable farming (Arko-Achemfuor et al. 2019). The research team met with the chief and community members through attending the community meetings to obtain feedback on their progress and their desires for the future. Through this process, several additional training opportunities were developed, including learning to develop and run a cooperative so they could sell their vegetables in their own communities. The farmers also started tending bee hives to harvest honey which had a naturally symbiotic relationship with the bees being there to pollinate the plants. The interventions continue to evolve based on the data collected through the community meetings, economic indicators, and climate data (e.g., water table levels).

Lesego Serolong explicitly addressed the importance of challenging versions of reality that sustain an oppressive status quo. The area in which this project was undertaken was written off as one with no economic viability. However, Serolong saw the area as having untapped potential, real challenges, and strengths in Indigenous knowledge and connection to the land of the community members. This challenge to an oppressive reality with the visibility of a transformative reality is captured in these words:

These villages and their surrounding areas have vast arable lands that are not being fully utilized due to lack of adequate public investments. This can be regarded as presenting a great opportunity for growth and economic development within these communities. Hence, instead of reproducing ways of speaking which point to the non-viability of these communities in terms of economic thriving, Bokamoso is intent on forwarding a "version of reality" based on seeing (and activating) untapped potential in recognition that, as Mertens (2017, p. 21) reminds us, there are consequences associated with accepting one version of reality over another.

(Arko-Achemfuor et al. 2019: 8)

The Indigenous transformative approach to these seemingly intransigent problems has yielded transformative changes (McIntyre et al. 2019). Participants can now earn a sustainable livelihood as evidenced by the twenty-five farmers who completed the program becoming less dependent on social grants. Some of the farmers are participating in the cooperative and growing more produce for their households and community. Farmers are requesting additional training in topics such as computers and English. Goats were thriving on the local vegetation and discussions were underway to introduce milk-producing goats in order to provide an opportunity to make and sell cheese. The growing of watermelons looked promising until the temperatures soared and the farmers did not have a truck to take the watermelons to market. This is a setback, but through the ongoing collection of data and communication of concerns, these problems can be brought to the community to generate solutions. The transformation is most evident in the sustainability of this effort based on the strength of the community networks and the enthusiasm of the teams to pursue solutions and new innovations. As this study illustrates the Indigenous framing of a study requires flexibility and responsiveness and a willingness to change directions when data indicate that community members need something that was not initially known.

Indigenous Mixed Methods Case Study #2: Health Disparities and Native Americans

A second example of an Indigenous mixed methods approach also invokes an Indigenous/transformative lens to study health disparities experienced by Native Americans (Lucero et al. 2018). The researchers explained that their approach "integrated a mixed methodology at all stages of the research process, often revisiting stages to incorporate new knowledge gained from practice. We refer to this as an iterative integration approach, in which our interdisciplinary team was grounded in an indigenous-Transformative paradigm that recognized different ways of knowing at each stage and at critical decision points" (57). Thus, their design was cyclical (revising stages to incorporate new knowledge) and included parallel (quantitative and qualitative data at the same time) and sequential collection (one type of data collection followed by another type of data collection). They described their design as a cyclical parallel and sequential mixed methods type.

Three issues were identified as being relevant to the ongoing health disparities in Native American communities: lack of trust in research conducted in their communities, small numbers of scientists from their communities, and lack of rigorous research to address health disparities (Lucero et al. 2018). A Native American Research Center for Health, a collaboration between the Indian Health Service and the National Institutes of Health, received a three-year grant to address these three issues. This was followed by a four-year grant to test the theory that community-based participatory research added value in research related to health disparities. *"Research for Improved Health (RIH): A Study of Community-Academic Partnerships* was a 4-year (2009–2013) study funded by the National Institutes of Health (NIH) and co-led by the National Congress of American Indians Policy Research Center, the University of New Mexico Center for Participatory Research, and the University of Washington, Indigenous Wellness Research Institute" (56). This inclusive partnership at the beginning of the study is indicative of the value placed on relationships that is part of both the Indigenous and the Transformative paradigms. The goal of the research was to identify criteria for successful community-based participatory research partnerships that were associated with reduced health disparities in Native American communities.

The researchers were very explicit about the components of their design (Lucero et al. 2018):

- Contextual analysis of socioeconomic status, history of Native American communities, institutional racism, culture, political policies, access to funding, history of collaboration between communities and academics, capacity of the partners, and health issues.

- Relationship building that included a focus on structural dynamics such as diversity, complexity, sharing power; individual dynamics such as core values, motivations, cultural identity, spirituality, and humility; and relational dynamics such as trust, safety, language, leadership, power dynamics, and participatory decision-making.

- Intervention and research design that included determining the cultural fit, being informed by the local settings and organizations, reflecting partnership inputs, and engagement with community members in all research activities.

- Outcomes such as changes in policies and practices, sustainable culturally responsive interventions, changed power relations, productivity measures (papers, grant applications, and awards), capacity development, and improved health, social and economic conditions, and reduced health disparities.

During the pilot project, a mixed methods design was used (Lucero et al. 2018). It included qualitative methods such as literature review and discussions with an advisory council made up of community and academic representatives, a quantitative web-based survey to determine the appropriateness of the components of the community-based participatory research model, followed by six qualitative community focus groups with local and national partnerships. For the follow-up study, the researchers consciously adopted the Indigenous and Transformative paradigms to frame their work. The Indigenous paradigm was reflected in their stance toward decolonizing the research by acknowledging historical abuses and honoring cultural strengths and community knowledge. Community members held power in the research process to inform the research process and bring their Indigenous knowledge into all aspects of the study. This aligns with both the Indigenous and Transformative paradigms as a way to support transformations that are valued by the communities. The researchers explained the intersection of the two paradigms this way: "While CBPR [Community Based Participatory Research] as a whole has adopted transformative ideas of endorsing community partners as knowledge co-creators and of applying research findings toward social justice, indigenous methodologies add more focused attention to culturally driven epistemologies and community control over research, such as ensuring Tribal (or community) data ownership after research is completed" (60).

The inclusion of the Indigenous lens led researchers to scrap their initial research design to start with a quantitative survey while simultaneously conducting case studies in six to eight communities (Lucero et al. 2018). At the beginning of the study, researchers asked the case study members to provide a timeline of their partnership experiences. The Native American participants voiced that their partnership with the government started hundreds of years ago when the federal army took their lands and destroyed their villages. This historical perspective led to discussions of how the interventions could be grounded to address historic inequities. Thus, the study took on a sequential form with the qualitative case studies being conducted first and their results providing a basis for a more culturally relevant and responsive quantitative survey. Furthermore, the case studies were then conducted not in the one-off style as initially planned, but as ongoing opportunities to consult with the community to gain deeper insights. Ongoing communication was essential to ensure conceptual alignment and responsiveness to communities. The research team leaders held monthly calls to talk about philosophical and conceptual integration. Members of the quantitative and qualitative teams engaged in more frequent meetings (weekly) to ensure their work was integrating the cultural and transformative concepts.

The data collection instruments and methods were summarized by Lucero and colleagues:

> The final Quantitative instruments included (1) a web-based Key Informant Survey completed by the CBPR Principal Investigator (PI) that featured questions related to project level facts, such as funding, years of partnering, partner member demographics, and so on; and (2) a web-based Community Engaged Survey that included perceptions of partnering quality, such as trust, power-sharing, governance, and multiple CBPR and health outcomes, mapped to the CBPR conceptual model domains. The final Qualitative case study instruments included (1) an individual interview guide, (2) a focus group guide, (3) a template for observation of a project partnership meeting, (4) a template for capturing historical timelines and social world map, and (5) a brief partner survey.
>
> (Lucero et al. 2018: 62)

Integration of the qualitative and quantitative data occurred at several stages of the study (Lucero et al. 2018). As already discussed, the structure of the quantitative instruments was informed by the results of the early case study data. Ongoing discussions between teams continued the integration throughout the process of implementing the study. At the data analysis stage, the researchers compared the quantitative and qualitative findings to co-validate (triangulate) the added value of CBPR in this context. They developed matrices that allowed them to compare the quantitative and qualitative findings with regard to relevant constructs such as trust and governance. The quantitative data on trust revealed that there were different levels of trust at the beginning of the partnerships. The qualitative data indicated that if people had a history of working together, then they had higher levels of trust. They also revealed that community members had suspicions about equity and power sharing. The partners also described how they increased in their feelings of trust when they were part of a process that allowed for critical reflection and their concerns were taken seriously. This building of trust is a critical component of the Indigenous and Transformative paradigms; the authentic application of the paradigms was witnessed in the changes made to the design and instrumentation based on input from the community. The use of the Indigenous and Transformative paradigms led to consciously seeking equity and social justice through respectful and reflective relationships that were informed by the specific histories of Indigenous people.

Indigenous Mixed Methods Case Study #3: Environmental Justice and Māori

Māori scholars have made major contributions to defining Indigenous approaches to research through their development of Kaupapa Māori (by Māori, for Māori) evaluation approaches (Chouinard and Cram 2020; Cram 2015; Smith 2012). A third example of Indigenous mixed methods research was conducted by Henwood and Henwood (2011), who used this framework to inform their design, implementation, and use of mixed methods research to document how the Māori community worked to restore a lake in their community after it had suffered from an environmental collapse due to excessive algal bloom. The ethical values were described as valuing the connection between humans and land and natural resources in which the health of one depends on the health of the other. This lake has significance for the Māori community because it has been a traditional source of food and is a resource that has economic, cultural, and spiritual value.

Henwood and Henwood (2011) recognized the diversity of stakeholders in their study: "the Lake Ömäpere Trust (who has legal title to the lake bed), mana whenua [people with customary authority over the land], local authorities, environmentalists, livestock farmers bordering the lake, the downstream communities of Utakura and the wider population connected to the Hokianga Harbour" (221). The contextual analysis included collection of data on the history of the area, the government regulations, land policies, legislation, farming practices, water quality monitoring data, and cultural and physical effects of the pollution of the lake on the Mäori people. They made use of a quantitative instrument developed by Mäori scholars to measure a Mäori cultural health index.

The Lake Ömäpere Project Management Group took the lead in the development of a collaborative that included the Lake Ömäpere Trust, two tribal councils, the Department of Conservation, and tribal representatives with expertise in environmental planning (Henwood and Henwood 2011). This collaborative reached out to other relevant groups, such as tribal collectives, livestock farmers, and local colleges and universities. Their interactions revealed different versions of reality. For example, the livestock farmers worried that the lake restoration activities would have a negative impact on their business and production. The Mäori owners wanted to restore the lake in order to reinstate the traditional economic and cultural resources that the lake originally held for them. An intervention was developed that was framed by these values: cultural and scientific knowledge, control and responsibility, unity of purpose, participation, collective strength, strategic alliances, and the health and wellbeing of the waters and the community. Thus, the collaborative worked with farmers to change farming practices to avoid contamination of the lake. Land owners and volunteers built fences along the lake to keep animals out of it and planted species of plants to restore the lake border.

Transformative changes in the lake were evident in the water quality data, fish count surveys, and strengthened relationships. "Working together and sharing skills and knowledge has created a broader awareness of environment and has led to offers of practical help from organizations and individuals (national and international), opportunities to build community data collection and analysis capability and invitations to present information about the lake at national and international conferences and seminars" (Henwood and Henwood 2011: 229). This approach reflects the benefits of building toward sustainability for complex problems. The integration of the quantitative and qualitative data allowed the researchers to be responsive to the information needs of diverse constituencies and document changes in processes and outcomes.

Indigenous Mixed Methods Case Study #4: Mental Health Services and Canadian Indigenous Youth

A fourth example of an Indigenous mixed methods study focuses on the engagement of Indigenous youth in urban settings to address inequities in mental health services in Canada (Bird-Naytowhow, Hatala, Pearl, Judge, and Sjoblom 2017). The researchers were explicit in the assumptions that guided their work, prioritizing spirituality and the well-being of the whole person and recognizing knowledge as being relational. They engaged with the tribal council for ethical review and they assured the tribe that the tribe would be the owners of the data at the end of the study. The researchers deliberately built relationships with the youth, community members, parents, elders, and community-based organizations. They established a community advisory committee that included Indigenous youth, elders, and parents. The youth acted as co-researchers and were able to influence the purpose and implementation of the research study. "Bringing Indigenous or spiritual values to the forefront of the research process—that is, qualities like respect, humility, reverence, kindness, or compassion—ensured that what was being done to generate knowledge about Indigenous youth resilience and wellness (i.e., research methodology) was being done in a good way, thereby safeguarding community relationships throughout the research process" (5).

Their contextual analysis focused on the history of colonization and systematic marginalization of Indigenous people. Extant data revealed inequities in the health system in the form of higher risks of alcoholism, drug use, and suicide, as well as disparities in economic status and access to power in policymaking. Proper Indigenous protocols were used before every meeting and data collection opportunity in the form of gifts of tobacco and smudging using sage. The data collection was done using photo voice and interviews. The youth took pictures at four different times of the year (four seasons) that depicted aspects of their lives that related to wellness and resilience. These photos then served as a basis for interviews conducted in the form of talking circles where the youth could share their stories and experiences. The talking circles were structured around the Medicine Wheel with four quadrants representing emotional, mental, physical, and spiritual parts of a person. This provision of a culturally safe space to discuss their problems and opportunities supported transformative capacity building for the youth who developed skills in using photovoice, participated in data collection and analysis, and presented their stories at various conferences. Community presentations and a three-week art exhibition of their photos opened up other opportunities to play a role in the transformation of their communities. "Having a 'transformative' vision of research is crucial to ensuring the project meaningfully engages with and can have direct benefit to the youth collaborators and was central to our intentions of carrying out research that would have a direct benefit to the youth involved" (6). Integration of the quantitative and qualitative data presented a powerful picture of the health inequities in this community and opened opportunities for positive transformations that are culturally responsive.

Indigenous Mixed Methods Case Study #5: Child Welfare Policy and Māori

A final Indigenous mixed methods study is reviewed here because it exemplifies a very different approach to the conduct of research through the use of big data. The New Zealand Ministry of Social Development commissioned a study to examine the feasibility of using predictive risk modeling to inform child welfare policy (Wilson and Cram 2018). Essentially, predictive risk modeling consists of calculating a statistical relationship between risk and protective factors and specific outcomes of interest, in this case the risk of child maltreatment. The use of predictive risk modeling to identify children most at risk was considered to be rather controversial in that "false positives" might result in stigmatization of families, children might be removed from their family homes, and Māori families might be over-represented and then subjected to additional surveillance. The researchers used two ethical review boards: one governmental and one tribal. The Māori ethical review made clear that ethical approval is not a "one and done"; rather, ethics requires ongoing engagement with the Māori community throughout the full process of the research. "This review emphasized the importance of an appropriate and acceptable service response for Māori, the need for engagement and consultation with Māori, and for trialling to establish whether benefits outweighed risks" (4).

The quantitative method used was analysis of linked de-identified administrative data across various government agencies (Wilson and Cram 2018). The researchers tested various algorithms for their accuracy in predictive modeling. A qualitative component was added in the form of a collaborative project controlled by the Māori community that examined the over-representation of Māori children. "A collaborative investigation of the feasibility study data was unable to confirm whether the representation of Māori children was proportionate to their real share of harm, and highlighted the contribution of wider inequities that have deep historic and structural roots to their over-representation" (10). The results of the collaborative inquiry were shared with a Māori advisory expert group who stated that predictive modeling might be feasible, but it should not replace the exercise of professional judgment. Integration of qualitative culturally responsive data throughout the study combined with the strong quantitative component led to the Indigenous community trusting the process and recommending additional action. The Minister of Social Development subsequently funded an additional research study to test how the predictive modeling data could be integrated into a call center where social workers make decisions when they receive a report of concern about a child. This study is underway.

The Indigenous paradigm leads to the development of mixed methods studies that prioritize relational ethics, spirituality, and connection to the land. Issues of discrimination and the legacy of colonization are highlighted and kept at the center of the investigation in order to consciously address traditional power inequities. Cultural protocols are followed in interactions with members of the Indigenous communities and the leaders of the research teams are from the communities. Problems are understood from the perspective of the community in ways that integrate Indigenous knowledge and data collected using culturally responsive strategies. Interventions are developed based on the Indigenous knowledge and data collected; often the interventions are evolving and changing based on findings during earlier phases of the study. In the next section, the Dialectical Pluralism meta-paradigm framework is discussed and illustrated using case studies.

Dialectical Pluralism and Mixed Methods

Dialectical Pluralism (DP) is different from the other philosophical paradigms that are described in this chapter. It is viewed as a meta-paradigm (Greene and Caracelli 1997; Johnson 2012; Johnson and Schoonenboom 2015). A researcher

> who works from a stance of DP is more likely to work with a team of [researchers] with a mixture of philosophical paradigms. The mixed methods (MM) DP [researcher's] role is to provide a respectful forum where multiple voices can be brought into decisions about the [research] questions and study design as well as in the data collection analysis, interpretation, and use phases of the study.
>
> (Mertens 2018: 22)

Researchers who work with a DP stance adopt a "both/and" mentality, holding that the integrity of each paradigm needs to be preserved and then brought in to conversation (dialogue) with each other.

Johnson (2012) provided the following description of the DP approach to mixed methods:

- Dialectically and dialogically listen, carefully and thoughtfully to different paradigms, disciplines, theories, and stakeholder and participant perspectives.

- Combine important ideas from competing paradigms and values into a workable whole for each research study.

- State and "pack" the approach with stakeholders' and researchers epistemological and social/political values to set the socially constructed standards and guide the research. This includes the valued ends one hopes for and the valued means for getting there.

- Try to reach at least some agreement among different researchers/practitioners on valued ends and means.

- Facilitate understanding, dissemination, and use of research findings (locally and more broadly).

- Continually, formatively evaluate and improve the outcomes of the research and use processes to have local and larger societal impacts (cited in Mertens 2018: 22–3).

The dialogue between data sets is the critical characteristics of the DP approach. "This conversational process requires a researcher adept at switching between two different paradigmatic perspectives and/ or one competent in seeing the sum of disparate parts. The ability to make these transitions between perspectives is identified by Johnson (2015) as fundamental to the dialectic stance" (Cronenberg 2020: 29). The DP approach to mixed methods has been used in a number of different sectors with different combinations of paradigms coming into conversation with each other.

Case Studies of the Dialectical Pluralism Approach to Mixed Methods

Dialectical Pluralism Mixed Methods Case Study #1: Dance/Movement Therapy

A DP approach to mixed methods is illustrated by Shim and colleagues (2021) through the use of a grounded theory approach combined with a quasi-experimental design mixed methods study of pain management through dance/movement therapy (DMT) in the United States. Traditionally, grounded theory is a methodology that is predominately qualitative and is conducted in order to systematically generate a theory (Glaser and Strauss 1967). Shim et al. labeled their design as an exploratory-confirmatory mixed methods grounded theory design (see Figure 2.6). This design

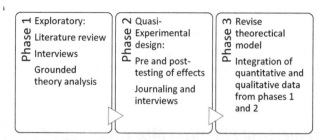

FIGURE 2.6 *Dialectical Pluralism Exploratory-Confirmatory Mixed Methods Grounded Theory Design (Adapted from Shim et al. 2021).*

differs from traditional grounded theory because of the inclusion of both qualitative and quantitative data and having a theory-testing phase. The researchers also used a quasi-experimental design within the mixed methods study to test the theoretical model they had developed in the grounded theory phase of the study. The research question was: "What theoretical model, grounded in qualitative and quantitative data, explains the therapeutic factors and mechanisms of DMT for resilience building in people living with chronic pain?" (Shim et al. 2021: 65).

In the first phase of their study, the exploratory part of the design was implemented through a literature review to identify models of how people who experience chronic pain build resilience through dance/movement therapy (Shim et al. 2021). This phase also included building a grounded theory based on the analysis of interview data that resulted in a second model for the same phenomenon. Data from the literature review and the interviews were integrated in order to produce a meta-model. The quasi-experimental design (one-group repeated measures design) consisted of pre- and post-testing of the effectiveness of participating in a DMT program. The quantitative measures focused on effectiveness indicators; the researchers also collected qualitative data during this phase through participant journaling and interviews. The integration of the qualitative and quantitative data informed the next stage of the study.

The grounded theory method was used again after the intervention to revise the theoretical model. The DP approach is evident in their description of this process: "The findings from Phase 1 and its resulting meta-model ... were compared against the findings from the Phase 2 clinical experiment-based model based on the MM quasi-experiment ...; then, through the meta-modeling process of comparison, integration, and refinement, the final theoretical model was produced" (Shim et al. 79).

Dialectical Pluralism Mixed Methods Case Study #2: Outdoor Play

Bhuyan and Zhang (2020) provide a second example of the DP approach in mixed methods through their study of children's play in Bangladesh that combined a constructivist phase with a pragmatic phase. The first phase used interviews with children and parents to "explore differential constructions of play and play space with reference to themes such as children's perceptions and preferences of play and play spaces, degree of independent mobility, perceptions on neighborhood environments, and so on" (361). The interview data were supplemented by children's drawings of their dream play spaces. The researchers also used surveys at this stage to collect demographic data and information about the amount of time children spent playing in different locations. The data from phase one were analyzed to identify themes around play and play spaces using grounded theory methods.

Buhyan and Yang (2020) used data from phase one to inform their methodology for the second pragmatic phase. They selected play spaces for systematic observations, defined context-specific spatial qualities of a play space, and developed quantitative indicators for statistical analysis of maps and GIS data. They used a quantitative instrument to record their systematic observations. They added interviews with the children to identify their preferred location for play (home or other play spaces such as playgrounds parks, and green spaces) and the accessibility of play spaces based on how far it was from home and the transportation needed to get there. The GIS data were used to depict the geometric configuration of the play spaces. The results indicated that children play for longer periods of time if the play space is enclosed and if there are small businesses in the street in front of the play space. Children also play longer in spaces that are nearer to their homes and that can be reached by walking.

The DP aspect of the study was evident in the use of a constructivist approach in the first phase with a pragmatic approach in the second phase, keeping the integrity of each paradigm intact. It is also evident in the conversation between the two phases of the study that occurred at the interpretation stage in the comparison of differential results from the interviews in phase one with the observations in phase two. For example, in the interviews, the difference between boys' and girls' preferences for playing outdoors was 18 percent; however, observations revealed an 82 percent difference in use of the outdoor play spaces.

Dialectical Pluralism Mixed Methods Case Study #3: Yoga and Cancer Patients

Leal and colleagues (2018) used a DP mixed methods approach, combining a Post-Positivist randomized control trial with a constructivist approach in their study of the effects of a yoga intervention for cancer patients in the United States. They described their DP approach as follows: "Dialectical pluralism combines the pragmatic recognition of the existence of multiple realities and perspectives embodied by quantitative and qualitative approaches, with a dialectical stance reliant on learning from the juxtaposition of differences, acknowledging the complementary nature of these two methods" (34). The constructivist approach was used to understand the psychological dynamics of patients with cancer as a process over time. These data were collected through written narratives produced by the cancer patients. The Post-Positivist approach was used to compare quality-of-life quantitative indicators using several standardized instruments for patients who participated in a yoga treatment with a control group.

Leal et al. (2018) collected quantitative and qualitative data concurrently (at roughly the same time points). The integrity of the two paradigmatic approaches (Constructivist and Pragmatic) was respected. Quantitative data collection included attention to internal and external validity, blinding of data collectors and analysts, and statistical methods of analysis. The qualitative data's rigor was enhanced by a transparent audit trail, researcher triangulation, peer debriefing, and use of direct quotations. Initial data analyses occurred separately for the quantitative and qualitative data. The differences between experimental and control groups were examined based on the quantitative data. Then the qualitative data were analyzed to identify recurrent themes. The conversations between the two occurred during data collection, analysis, and interpretation. The qualitative data were "quantitized" by counting the recurrent themes in each group. These "quantitized" qualitative data were then compared with the quantitative outcomes for the two groups. When discrepancies occurred between the two data sets, the researchers returned to the data to seek clarification of the findings. They described the benefits of using a DP approach as follows:

At the points where the data sets corresponded, integrating qualitative and quantitative data elucidated each, resulting in a synergistic and enriched understanding of patterns across time. Where they diverged, contextualizing quantitative data within participant's narratives allowed for the clarification of discrepancies, making inconsistencies between the various quantitative measures intelligible … The expression of congruence and divergence between the quantitative and qualitative data sets also reveals the reality and nuances of participants' cancer experiences. Although our study participants may exhibit overall positive or negative psychological adjustment on quantitative measures, their words tell us a deeper and at times a contradictory story. Embedding participants' qualitative narratives within a Tibetan yoga RCT provided the context that granted meaning to their isolated and abstract scores.

(Leal et al. 2018: 49)

The three Dialectical Pluralism examples illustrate how researchers work with two different paradigms, while keeping the assumptions of each intact. The combinations here included Constructivist, Pragmatic, and Post-Positivist. The important characteristic of note in Dialectical Pluralism studies is the conversation that occurs across paradigms in order to generate an understanding that surpasses what a single research approach can provide.

Summary

Paradigms are sets of philosophical assumptions that guide researchers in their methodological choices. Five paradigms (Post-Positivist, Constructivist, Pragmatic, Transformative, and Indigenous) and one meta-paradigm (Dialectical Pluralism) provide frameworks for decisions about mixed methods that influence the development of research questions, engagement with stakeholders and planning, implementation, and use of research strategies and findings. Sample studies were provided that illustrated the influence of the different frameworks for application of mixed methods in research. The examples come from diverse geographic regions (e.g., Malaysia, South Africa, England, United States, Canada, Cameroon, India, New Zealand, and Bangladesh) and multiple topics, such as environmental education, intimate partner violence, teacher and student stress, mindfulness training, dementia, imagery used by athletes, food emergencies, parenting, health services efficiency, school disparities, health services for sexual minorities, spinal cord injuries, agricultural sustainability, mental health services, child welfare policy, dance therapy, children's play, and yoga with cancer patients.

The assumptions of the Post-Positivist paradigm resulted in quantitatively dominant mixed methods designs and focused on determining the effectiveness of interventions. The constructivist assumptions led to an emphasis on qualitative data collection in a mixed methods design to understand the nature of participants' experiences. The Pragmatic paradigmatic assumptions were best suited when a practical question needed both quantitative and qualitative data to be answered. This was applied in settings to solve problems such as how to provide food services more efficiently and to reduce teacher stress. The Transformative paradigm's assumptions led to a more cyclical approach to mixed methods design, with a phase for building relationships and coalitions, and a phase for contextual analysis to understand relevant legislative, historical, economic, and educational conditions. The Indigenous paradigm's assumptions also resulted in a more cyclical approach with relationship building and contextual analysis; however, the process was more fluid and was allowed to emerge over time in response to community needs. In Dialectical Pluralism, the mixed methods designs tended to have a clearer separation of the quantitative parts of the design and the qualitative parts in order to preserve the integrity of the relevant paradigmatic assumptions that framed the studies.

Questions for Further Thinking:

1. What are the essential assumptions associated with the five paradigms (Post-Positivist, Constructivist, Pragmatic, Transformative, and Indigenous) and one meta-paradigm (Dialectical Pluralism)? Sketch out your understandings of each framework.
2. How would you describe the differences in the methodological choices under each of the paradigms and the meta-paradigm?
3. What do you see as the advantages and disadvantages of working within each framework?
4. Where would you situate yourself in the paradigmatic frameworks? Do you gravitate toward one or another? What is your reason for feeling more "at home" with one framework or another?

CHAPTER THREE

Becoming a Mixed Methods Researcher

Becoming a mixed methods researcher is challenging because of the dominance of specific methodologies within different disciplines and because of the traditional way of teaching research methods and socializing students into their professions:

> Disciplines in humanities, hard and social sciences; the arts; and other fields are distinct with their own intellectual histories, literatures, methodological conventions, and knowledge dissemination pathways. Researchers during their graduate training are socialized almost exclusively into their disciplines with little or no encouragement to immerse themselves in other disciplines. They delve deeply into the published literature associated with their specializations and master research methods and techniques regarded as most appropriate for scholars within their disciplinary domains. They eventually form and join discipline-bordered professional groups set off by distinctive viewing positions, insider knowledge, and other in-group understandings.
>
> (Hemmings, Beckett, Kennerly and Yap 2013: 263)

Research training in academia has traditionally been discipline based. Given that quantitative methods dominate in some disciplines and qualitative methods dominate in others, the process of becoming a mixed methods researcher will be different depending on your discipline and its history with methodologies. If your expertise is largely in either quantitative or qualitative methods, you might choose to form a research team with other researchers who have skills that complement your own. Whether you decide to bolster your skill base as a way to incorporate mixed methods or decide to go with the team approach, it is useful to know the basics of how to design and conduct a mixed methods study. Fortunately, many resources are available for training in mixed methods such as books, workshops, webinars, and professional associations; these are presented later in this chapter.

Tessa Muncey, the pioneer in mixed methods research who was introduced in Chapter 1, reflected on how she and her students came to learn about mixed methods when it was not yet in any textbooks. Her disciplinary base was in nursing where randomized control trial designs dominated. She acknowledged the usefulness of RCTs when the goal was to count things and to answer questions about what treatments works. She also noted: "When you are looking after people, there are many 'why' questions: Why doesn't it work? Or, how did it feel to have one treatment or another? This required balancing quantitative and qualitative data in the same study. My students wanted to interview their participants to find out more about why" (Interview of Tessa Muncey conducted by Donna Mertens, July 2021). She noted that initially the students used designs that were predominantly RCTs with interviews until the mixed methods books started coming out, and they found encouragement to be more creative in their designs. Her experience in teaching mixed methods research was reinforced by the acknowledgment that complex problems require interdisciplinary teams to effectively address them, thus raising the need of learning to work across disciplines for mixed methods researchers.

The dominance of the Post-Positivist paradigm in health sciences is explained in historical terms by Michael Fetters, pediatrician and editor of the *Journal of Mixed Methods Research*:

> At least in my generation, I don't think it's that much different now, it's just there is only one science; there's only one way of viewing the world, which is a measurement world ... with the strongest evidence always being a randomized control trial, and

that was an experimental design and some kind of a systematic review and they've just seen a case study as essentially worthless. (Interviewed by Donna Mertens, October 2021)

I asked Fetters what he suggested was needed to transform disciplines from a strongly quantitative stance to a mixed methods stance, thus opening doors for mixed methods training in these disciplines. He said that he starts by making a careful argument for the benefits of the inclusion of qualitative data in language that will be understood by the medical community. "Acknowledging that there would be people that might not know what the terminology was and to educate the audience; that's what I found to be the most effective way for writing proposals or for writing papers." The growing acceptance of mixed methods in the health field is visible in the new guidelines for funding and conducting research that were reviewed in Chapter 1. Fetters further commented on the shift in the research community's acceptance of mixed methods because of the new guidelines:

We're looking at this as a new level of maturity of the field to see how many organizations now provide guidance and recommendations, so that means that they're expecting that their constituencies have an interest in this, and there are key stakeholders who have an interest, and if the methods are to be used, this is what they want them to do and how they want them to use them.

(Interview with Donna Mertens, October 2021)

Fetters noted that this shift in guidance is being accompanied by increased interest across disciplines in the use of mixed methods, with implications for training mixed methods researchers. Many researchers are trained in one method such as RCTs but they find that funders are requiring mixed methods designs. Researchers who are entering the field need to figure out how to receive training in mixed methods. Some professional organizations are offering guidance in designing high-quality mixed methods studies such as:

the American Psychological Association (APA) included qualitative and quantitative and mixed methods in their newest published guidelines, because APA had previous methodology guidelines. These were additions to their old guidelines. It almost makes me think that the mixed methods made it easier to pick up the qualitative because the mixed methods is acknowledging the value of that quantitatively focused aspect of work in which they have a great interest. And that it's almost like this stepping stone to include qualitative.

(Michael Fetters, interviewed by Donna Mertens,
October 2021)

Thus far, this chapter described challenges in the preparation of mixed methods researchers and touched on strategies for opening pathways for the acceptance of mixed methods research in various disciplines. The shift in guidelines across multiple professional organizations and funding agencies adds to the importance of the inclusion of mixed methods and the ability to use these methods. As mentioned earlier, mixed methods research can be conducted by researchers who are expert in mixed methods; they can also be conducted by teams of researchers, each of whom has expertise in different methodologies. In the latter case, the researchers need to develop sufficient understanding of mixed methods to work together in a fruitful manner.

Academic Coursework and Professional Development in Mixed Methods

Knowledge about mixed methods in research has expanded greatly over the last two decades. Hence, it is important to look at mechanisms for teaching mixed methods research that is more than a single module added to a sequence of methodology courses (Mertens et al. 2016). Knowing the different paradigmatic frameworks that are guiding thinking in mixed methods is important so that mixed methods researchers understand the assumptions that guide their methodological choices (Mertens 2010). Researchers can review examples of mixed methods research that illustrate different paradigmatic assumptions in operation and come to understand the influence of these assumptions on the development of research questions, designs, and plans for data collection, analysis, and use.

There are different views in the mixed methods community as to the best sequence of courses for teaching mixed methods. One argument holds that students should take quantitative methods course and qualitative methods courses to build a foundation from which to take courses in mixed methods. Another argument holds that students should be led by their research interests and then be provided with opportunities to learn the methodologies that have relevance for them to answer their research questions. Pat Bazeley, president of the Mixed Methods International Research Association Oceana Chapter in 2021, commented on the importance of starting with the focus of the research as a decision point for how to teach research methods. She recommends starting with the research problem and encouraging students to think creatively about different ways they could address the problem. As the student becomes clearer about the necessary methods, they can take training in the relevant methods. She said:

> Some problems are better addressed using text, visual, or sound type of data and some that are more oriented toward numeric data ... If you start from that point (a wholistic way), integration is natural ... Then what you can do is have modular add-ons, if you want to run an experiment, run a module on experimental design. You can do a modular thing on statistical analysis or sampling theory or text analysis. Build those in as modules around the core which is an integrated approach ... I want to engender a way of thinking about things that contextualize them so they are considered in their whole.
>
> (Interview with Pat Bazeley by Donna Mertens, October 2021)

The use of modules specific to a research interest has merit; however, researchers also need to consider how they develop the depth of knowledge in skills in quantitative and qualitative methods as a basis for the integration of the methods. This is the position of Creswell and Plano Clark (2011) and discussed by Kong et al. (2018) in their study presented in Chapter 2 on environmental education. They had skills in both qualitative and quantitative methods and augmented these skills by "attending methodological workshops, reading published MMR [Mixed Methods Research] studies, and locating literature syntheses of many MMR studies in particular fields" (160). They also identified experts in mixed methods research with whom they discussed their research design and implementation.

Two universities in Texas (the University of Texas School of Public Health and Texas A&M School of Rural Public Health) and their community-based partner provide another option for new mixed methods researchers to consider. They developed a doctoral level mixed methods seminar that focused on the integration of mixed methods and community-based participatory research (CBPR) (Upadhyaya, May, and Highfield 2015). The seminar began with two parallel activities: building interdisciplinary teams and learning about the ontological and epistemological assumptions in mixed methods research. Academic teaching continued throughout the seminar in the form of lectures, exercises, presentations, and group discussions to teach the students about CBPR and mixed methods theory and design. This was followed by a period of time being devoted to building relationships between the participants (students) and the community that would be engaged with during their research through meetings, brainstorming sessions, and webinars. The result of these activities was the development of research objectives, questions, methods, and rationale that were based on the community input, in accordance with the CBPR approach. The students then developed research proposals that depicted how they would integrate CBPR and mixed methods based on the community partner's interests. These proposals were then shared with students, faculty, and community members for review and feedback. Students revised their proposals to respond to the feedback; they could use these proposals to conduct research through an additional seminar or as dissertation projects. "The iterative process needed to create a final unified draft from the two drafts compelled students to integrate and practice principles of team science (i.e., mutual respect, power balance, and effective communication) and CBPR (i.e., shared knowledge and resources) to arrive at an actionable solution to the problem at hand" (289).

The Universitas Padjadjaran (UnPad) in Indonesia West Java offers a unique model for training mixed methods researchers that focuses on the Transformative paradigm at the undergraduate, graduate, and postgraduate students, as well as a diploma program for government workers. Led by Dr. Ida Widianingsih, vice-dean for Learning, Research, and Student Affairs, the program sees the importance of transformative mixed methods because it presents a new model for engaging with university students and village youth in a research context to build their capacities. Her approach to teaching mixed methods research provides insights into strategies for building capacity through practical experience and theoretical teaching. The university has a program that includes community service and she combines training in mixed methods with that requirement. She said:

> I explain my research interest in environmental issues and give them data about the village we are working with. One group of the students decided to do a research project with primary school children on their understanding of environmental issues. The other group chose how to improve the quality of the food products of the women's group in the village. The students gather data online to formulate their approach to the intervention and research and then present it to the full class and the professor. After the plan was refined, I contacted the Head of the village about the primary school children project and ask his permission to work with the students in the village. I make it clear that we will support small transformations based on input from the head of the school and teachers, elders, and the village Head. With their agreement, UnPad provides reciprocity that enables the research to proceed by providing free Wi-Fi to the village.
> (Interview with Ida Widianingsih conducted by Donna Mertens, October 2021)

The transformative mixed methods approach used by Ida Widianingsih exemplifies the importance of the paradigmatic framework that researchers use. The quantitative data came from extant databases and gave a picture of the environmental and educational conditions in the village. The qualitative data were specifically designed to be appropriate for cultural expression by young students. Relationship building and adhering to cultural protocols is important. Reciprocity was provided to the village school in the form of free Wi-Fi and in the learning that the children gained. Sustainability was achieved because of good relationships and a positive experience in the process of the research. Both students and village members enhanced their mixed methods research skills through this practical experience.

Academic programs can be a great way to learn mixed methods; however, not all universities have developed these. Professionals who have completed their formal education for the most part have not had the opportunity to learn mixed methods and may not be in a position to return to academic classes. For this very large constituency, training programs offered through professional associations or funding organizations are an important resource for learning mixed methods.

Training in Mixed Methods through Professional Associations and Funding Agencies

Many professional associations such as the British Psychological Association, the American Educational Research Association, the British Educational Research Association, the European Evaluation Society, and the American Evaluation Association also have professional development opportunities to learn about mixed methods research. The Mixed Methods International Research Association and its affiliates provide workshops, in person and online, for people who want to learn the many different aspects of mixed methods. They offer monthly workshops on a variety of mixed methods research topics that are archived and can be accessed through their website. In addition, they have a series of modules formatted as Massive Open Online Courses that have been organized from beginning concepts through specialty topics, such as use of mixed methods in evaluation.

The NIH Office of Behavioral and Social Science Research funds several institutes under its Mixed Methods Research Training Program for the Health Sciences (Guetterman, Creswell, Deutsch, and Gallo 2019). The components of these year-long trainings include webinars, assignment of mentors to the participants, a website with additional resources, and an annual retreat.

The topics covered were an introduction to mixed methods, mixed methods designs, rigorous mixed methods components, becoming a resource, and an overview to prepare for the subsequent retreat ... The educational objective was that scholars would be able to explain fundamental concepts of mixed methods research and identify major elements of current mixed methods thinking to include in their project application. These elements included the justification, designs, diagrams, study aims, use of theory, sampling, integration strategies, rigorous qualitative and quantitative methods, interdisciplinary teams, evaluation topics, and strategies for writing mixed methods for proposals and articles.

(Guetterman et al. 2019: 56)

These trainings were designed to be experiential and result in the preparation of grant proposals that incorporated the use of mixed methods. The participants of the first training program noted the importance of learning about the integration of the quantitative and qualitative methods as they came to the training with expertise in individual methodologies.

Two additional aspects of becoming a mixed methods researcher are discussed in the next sections of this chapter: building research capacity in communities and building effective research teams.

Building Research Capacity in Communities

Mixed methods researchers need to understand what assumptions guide their methodological choices, as well as how they approach capacity building, especially with communities. Pohatu and Warmenhoven (2007) are members of the community in which they work: the Māori in New Zealand. Their goal in capacity building is to avoid the Eurocentric approaches to research in order to support the flourishing of Indigenous people and to meet the challenge of doing research as an "insider" in ways that honored the community priorities. They set out to build a research team within their rural Māori community in conjunction with the He Oranga mo nga Uri Tuku Iho Trust (the Trust), a collective of tribal members on the East Coast of New Zealand. Their description of building research capacity in these communities highlights the importance of paying attention to the voices of members of marginalized communities when conducting this type of training. It is not all about knowledge; relationship cultivation and nurturing in culturally responsive ways are crucial.

Capacity building of hapü [sub-tribe of descendants and families from a particular ancestor] members, including the twenty or so employees of the Trust over the last four years comprising of principal researchers, research assistants, administrators, advisors and trustees (a mix of elders, mature persons and youth) has been central to the programme through wananga [Māori space for academic learning and debate, transmission of knowledge], hui [meeting or gathering], workshops and training. Researchers use whakakotahitanga [to unite]—participatory processes from programme concept to completion as well as inclusive management structures to enable effective delivery to hapü and other end users. In addition, the trust is building and enhancing links between whanau [family], marae [members of a meeting house], hapü and iwi [tribe] including Wananga such as Awanuiarangi [a Māori initiated tertiary educational institution that offers coursework from entry-level university through PhD]. We have broadened our network into Universities, State governed Research Institutes and research foundations both nationally and internationally, and have come to value these relationships. Furthermore, we foster and maintain key contacts within local regional and central government agencies.

(Pohatu and Warmenhoven 2007: 111)

This culturally rooted approach to capacity building contributes to sustainability of research teams because it is respectful and integrated into the life of the community. The building of teams is a skill that is not included in all methodological textbooks, but it is important in mixed methods because of the need to work with researchers and community members with different skills, expertise, and experiences.

Challenges and Strategies for Mixed Methods Team Development

Mixed methods requires expertise in both quantitative and qualitative methods, as well as skill integrating those methods. Complex problems often require researchers from multiple disciplines in order to bring the expertise needed to solve problems. Hence development of expertise in mixed methods goes beyond methodological knowledge and includes how to work with interdisciplinary teams who may come to the study with different philosophical assumptions. Hesse-Biber (2016) raised this observation about interdisciplinary work:

> Researchers do not practice interdisciplinarity well. This is because, in part, they do not actively seek out ways to tap into the potential synergy of a team-based mixed methods project. They ethnocentrically do not see past their own comfort zone or horizon for theories, questions, and methods. I further argue that there is a lack of conscious reflexivity on the part of the research team; instead, the team often buys into the idea of "inherent" synergy contained in these types of research configurations and designs. Working in a group does not necessarily mean that you are working as a team.
>
> (224)

Bazeley (2018) highlighted the advantages of cross-disciplinary collaborations while also providing a cautionary tale when she wrote,

> Bringing researchers from different disciplines together in a project team accentuates epistemological, methodological, methods, and language differences …. Those from particular disciplines often lack understanding of research processes associated with alternative disciplines, including sampling analysis strategies, and interpretation. They have different understandings of what counts as evidence and what counts as quality, with different audiences, timelines, and publishing goals. These differences increase the potential for power games resulting in disagreement and delay. The "dysfunctional" team, with unresolved differences, will usually produce separate reports of project components and/or reduced overall output.
>
> (50)

The need for integrating quantitative and qualitative skills and the multi-disciplinary nature of mixed methods highlights the importance of developing the skills to build effective research teams in order to have the necessary knowledge and expertise. The examples presented in this section give us an opportunity to learn about different ways that researchers have addressed the challenges of building effective mixed methods research teams.

Curry, O'Cathain, Plano Clark, Aroni, Fetters, and Berg (2012) noted several challenges in building research teams: "(a) dealing with differences, (b) trusting the 'other', (c) creating a meaningful group, (d) handling essential conflicts and tensions, and (e) enacting effective leadership roles" (5). She and her colleagues conducted discussions among themselves over an eighteen-month period in order to analyze the challenges and strategies for addressing them. They emphasized the importance of creating a climate in which each team member's experience was respected, group members could speak candidly about their perspectives on the research study, allowing tensions to surface and be examined within a safe group context, and creating fluid leadership roles dependent on the stage of the study. Their work highlights the inevitability of tensions that go beyond methodology when diverse teams are brought together.

Claasen, Covic, Idsardi, Sandham, Gildenhuys, and Lemke (2015) faced challenges in their research on agricultural and nutrition programs in South Africa in which they built a transdisciplinary team of researchers, as well as engaged with community members throughout the research process. The researchers recognized that the complexity of research on sustainable diets in this context required expertise in nutrition, economics, agriculture, and behavioral, environmental, and social sciences. They chose a mixed methods design because: "Given the wide spectrum of factors that influence the concept of sustainable diets, transdisciplinary and mixed methods inquiry can support better the investigation of the whole spectrum of factors involved" (3). "A transdisciplinary research approach that encourages the fusion of knowledge as well as methodologies of different disciplines is essential to investigate the interrelated complexity of sustainable diets" (Classen et al. 2015:8). They described their research team composition and functioning as follows:

Regular team discussions ensured reflection on data collection, analysis, and interpretation (Classen et al. 2015). Experts from various disciplines formed the research team, including nutrition, agricultural economics, environmental science, law, consumer sciences, social sciences in agriculture, and social anthropology.

The research team further included two persons who live and work in the communities of the Vaalharts region, adding valuable local contextual knowledge for reflection. The team leader is a nutritionist experienced with qualitative and quantitative research inquiries. In addition, feedback to research participants forms an integral part of the analytical process so that their voices are embedded into data analysis and interpretation processes. This allows for more in-depth contextual reflection and interpretation, important to understanding the complex dimensions of sustainable diets that are mostly missing in standard study designs.

(Classen et al. 2015: 8)

The team worked together throughout the study to refine the research focus, design, and implementation. All team members participated in the data analysis. After each phase of data collection, feedback was given to community members, farmers, processors, and other key informants. The researchers reported that they experienced challenges with some of the experts who were not able to provide the time required for transdisciplinary work and in-depth discussions. This approach does require more time and resources for team meetings and for continuous community engagement. Kong et al. (2018) write that it is incumbent upon the researchers to make the case that the use of mixed methods can result in increased impact, and thus, is worth the extra time and resources.

Different kinds of challenges arise when teams from different cultural groups are brought together. This was the case with the UK government's Official Development Assistance Global Challenges Research Fund (GCRF) that was initiated to support the formation of Indigenous and non-Indigenous research partnerships (Edwards, Barnes, McGregor, and Brannelly 2020). Tensions were apparent in the beginning of the initiative because the UK government had already decided on the most important global challenges (i.e., sustainable development, good governance, and eradication of poverty). The GCRF documents actually placed the research expertise in the UK: "The GCRF will allow UK research excellence to be deployed in a strategic way to generate solutions to the most significant and complex problems faced by developing countries while at the same time strengthening their research capability" (UKRI [UK Research and Innovation] 2017b, unpaginated) (https://www.ukri.org/files/legacy/research/gcrf-strategy-june-2017/)" (cited in Edwards et al. 2020). This predetermined purpose of the partnerships while valuing the UK research knowledge over Indigenous knowledge set up the initiative to perpetuate historical exploitation.

A team of Indigenous and non-Indigenous researchers challenged the colonizing and oppressive nature of the GCRF and obtained funding through UKRI's International Collaboration Initiative through a grant made to the ESRC National Centre for Research Methods (Edwards et al. 2020). This team of Indigenous and non-Indigenous researchers partnered to produce resources for decolonizing research strategies that can meet the challenges in research partnerships. The resources they developed are available at a website: https://www.indigenous.ncrm.ac.uk/about/. Edwards and colleagues share the need for honest and frank conversations in research partnerships about the legacy of colonialism, the historical dominance of Western ways of knowing, and methods and approaches that are reflective of Indigenous research, values, and ways of collaborating. For example, they talk about how non-Indigenous researchers in partnership with Māori researchers cannot rush "the project without consulting with, listening to and respecting the knowledge and input of the Māori community, and how they go about doing this and working with their co-researcher" (9).

Hemmings, Beckett, Kennerly, and Yap (2013) provide insights into how researchers can learn to work together across disciplines and paradigms. The teams in their study were from nursing and education; the researchers documented how they addressed social dynamics to build an effective mixed methods research approach. They described the process of learning to work together as a "re-education" experience that included sharing readings that came from their respective disciplines and engaging in weekly discussions of this literature. The research member teams needed to take on an instructor's role in the beginning of the project. The team members experienced frustration when asked to move outside their comfort areas in terms of accepted methodologies, but they engaged in deliberate conversations to acknowledge this frustration and develop ways to work together. Hemmings et al. noted that this team building process was time consuming, but they argued that it is necessary in order to achieve the goals of working together in a mixed methods study. The essential characteristics of effective team dynamics included sharing mental models, developing trust, and having effective leadership.

Summary

Becoming a mixed methods researcher is a challenge because of the need to have expertise in quantitative and qualitative methods and skill in integrating those two methods. Traditional research methods training has been conducted within the approaches most commonly used in specific disciplines. Researchers who want to become mixed methods researchers can form teams with researchers whose skills complement their own. Many funding organizations and professional associations are now recommending the use of mixed methods; hence, researchers can take advantage of opportunities to develop their mixed methods skills through academic programs, journals, books, workshops, webinars, and professional development trainings. Mixed methods researchers need to understand the assumptions that guide their methodological decisions. Examples of training students, team members, and communities in mixed methods highlight the importance of capacity building as part of the process of developing high-quality mixed methods studies. Learning about strategies for working with teams is an important component of developing as a mixed methods researcher.

Questions for Further Thinking:

1. How is research taught in your discipline? Which types of methods are given preference (e.g., quantitative, qualitative, and mixed methods)?
2. How do you plan to enhance your mixed methods skills?
3. What experience have you had with working with research teams? How could the team dynamics be improved when mixed methods are used in the study?
4. What resources for building your mixed methods skills have you found at the MMIRA website or at your own professional association's website?

CHAPTER FOUR

The Future of Mixed Methods: Challenges and Innovations in Diverse Contexts

Mixed methods approaches offer researchers an exciting opportunity to explore new combinations of methods in diverse contexts. These opportunities are accompanied by theoretical and methodological challenges. Mixed methods design possibilities are endless and can be developed based on a number of different frameworks to align with researchers' assumptions. Thus, the field provides fertile ground for innovations and divergent thinking.

The Mixed Methods International Research Association established a task force to look into future challenges for the field; this resulted in an internal report and a published journal article (Mertens, Bazeley, Bowleg, Fielding, Maxwell, Molina-Azorin, and Niglas 2016). The task force members identified five major themes that represented opportunities and challenges for the mixed methods research community: advancing understandings of philosophy and methodology, development of innovative designs, incorporating technological advancements and big data, improving the preparation of mixed methods researchers, and increasing responsiveness to complex societal problems. Molina and Fetters (2018) presented a similar list of topics of future interest for mixed methods researchers: expanding understandings of paradigms, integration of methods, training mixed methods researchers, technological advances, building and using teams, and innovations in research designs, data collection, analysis, and use for social change.

Although the themes identified by the MMIRA task force (Mertens et al. 2016) were for a five-year period (2016–20), their relevance continues for the mixed methods research community, perhaps in a more nuanced way given the knowledge gained over time. Continued advances are replete with challenges. In this chapter, I discuss the following opportunities and challenges:

- The role of paradigms in mixed methods research: permeable borders

- Indigenous philosophical paradigm and mixed methods

- Creating effective relationships in mixed methods: inclusion of community voices

- Ethics and mixed methods

- Challenging traditional methodological practices to incorporate mixed methods

- Increasing the impact of mixed methods research: meeting grand challenges of social, economic, and environmental justice in order to be part of the solution for such societal challenges as the climate crisis; disparities in the economic, educational, and health systems; and global and regional conflicts, and pandemics

The Role of Paradigms in Mixed Methods Research: Permeable Borders

The concept of paradigms is one that has garnered much attention in the mixed methods research literature. This concept was used to organize the content in this book because it allows researchers to bring a critical eye to the assumptions that guide their methodological choices. Researchers who work from different assumptions articulate concerns about research approaches that differ from their own assumptions. For example, Hesse Biber (2015) raises questions for those who choose to use mixed methods about the assumption by researchers who are situated in the Pragmatic paradigm that the research question drives the choice of methods:

> Who gets to carve out and determine what knowledge becomes legitimated? To what extent does this process serve specific ends? What is lost? Who gets to challenge and reframe or rename a given concept? .... Just how the research question enters into the mixed methods research (MMR) project remains woefully unarticulated.
>
> (Hesse Biber 2015: 784)

Researchers new to mixed methods (or even those who have considerable experience) can reflect on these questions and decide on the processes they want to use in the formulation of research questions.

Fàbregues, Escalante-Barrios, Molina-Azorin, Hong, and Verd (2021) reported that the mixed methods researchers in their study were concerned about the mismatch between pragmatism as a philosophy and how it is portrayed as a framework for mixed methods research:

> The mixed methods community sometimes characterize the notion of pragmatism in a superficial way by reducing it to merely eclecticism and confusing it with "practicalism." In this way, these authors advocate a "what works" approach which may be useful when justifying the integration of the quantitative and qualitative methods, but this attitude distorts the nature of pragmatism by failing to consider its underlying theoretical and philosophical assumptions.
>
> (9)

Researchers entering the field of mixed methods can benefit from knowing about the different paradigms as well as reflecting on the criticisms of these paradigms.

The Transformative paradigm has been criticized as being too vague and open for interpretation (Sweetman, Badiee, and Creswell 2010). The complexity of the contexts and problems addressed in transformative mixed methods study prevent a step-by-step cookbook approach to applying this framework. As Garnett and colleagues (2019) noted in their study of school inequities, they viewed the vagueness of the transformative lens as a strength. "The intentional flexibility inherent in this paradigm creates space for interdisciplinary thinking, integration of various ways of knowing and questioning the processes of mixed methods research" (Garnett et al. 2019: 8) that they needed to adapt the research approach to meet the needs of the students who experienced discrimination in the school system.

Questions also arise as to the nature of the borders between the paradigms with some researchers suggesting that it was not possible to cross paradigmatic borders because of conflicting assumptions. For example if a Post-Positivist researcher holds that there is only one reality that can be measured with a certain amount of error, how can this be reconciled with the version of reality that is held by constructivists that reality is a socially constructed construct? Mixed methods researchers who adopt the stance of Dialectical Pluralism answer this question by asserting that researchers adhere to the assumptions of each paradigm that frames their work and then put the methods and findings into conversation with each other (dialectical). Other researchers write about the permeability of the borders between the paradigmatic frameworks, as was illustrated in Chapter 3 with case studies that integrated the Indigenous paradigm with the Transformative paradigm. The mixed methods community has been enlarged and enriched by the inclusion of the voices of Indigenous scholars and the meaning of Indigenous philosophical assumptions to guide methodological choices. This represents an opportunity and a challenge in the mixed methods community.

Indigenous Philosophical Paradigm and Mixed Methods

The Indigenous paradigm has only recently been included in the mixed methods literature and hence there is much to learn about its role here. This paradigm informs the research community of critically important issues when research is undertaken with Indigenous communities (Chilisa 2020; Chilisa and Mertens 2021). The examples of mixed methods using an Indigenous lens were presented in Chapter 3. However, the challenges that face the mixed methods community are highlighted here. First, Indigenous knowledge is not a new thing. Indigenous knowledge and ways of doing research have been characterized as being: "as old as the hills and the valleys, the mountains and the seas, and the deserts and the lakes that Indigenous people bind themselves to as their places of belonging" (Cram, Chilisa, and Mertens 2013: 11). The newness of this paradigm in the literature supports the concerns that members of Indigenous (and other marginalized communities) have been historically excluded and their knowledge not valued in the research world.

Many research studies aim to measure the effects of an intervention, with success being defined by the researchers. These measurements might be conceptualized as improvements in a targeted behavior, a change in attitudes, or a change in knowledge or skills. Indigenous scholars challenge us to think about success in broader terms that encompass the values placed on mind, body, and spirit, and the connections we share with each other and with nature (Pidgeon 2019). How can our understanding of mixed methods grow when we consider the whole person and connections with nature?

The Indigenous paradigm specifies the importance of honoring the culture of Indigenous communities, valuing Indigenous knowledge, and engaging with members of those communities as agents of change (Pidgeon 2019). As a research community, we can think about the extension of this approach when we work with other marginalized communities. Researchers worldwide can reflect on how to better understand the communities where they work and build relationships based on respect. It prompts us to ask the question: How can our research be "an active form of resistance to the oppressive, colonial representation of the past that resulted in inadequate policy, methodology, and theoretical applications against Indigenous peoples" (Pidgeon 2019: 422) and, by extension, in other communities in which we work? How can mixed methods be an asset in this regard?

The Indigenous paradigm also challenges us to think about the question raised by researchers in other contexts: Who can speak for the community? (Pidgeon 2019). For example, in Canadian Indigenous communities on-reserve or identified First Nation Communities, formal governance structures exist and must be respected. For Indigenous persons who live in urban areas, this formal structure may not be present. However, there are organizations such as Indigenous community centers or support systems in universities that can guide researchers in these contexts. This raises the question: To what extent do we seek out formal or organizational allies in our research in marginalized communities to determine how to be inclusive in culturally responsive ways?

Indigenous authors have also brought to visibility the concept of decolonizing research, which Thambinathan and Kinsella (2021) defined as: "Decolonizing research means centering concerns and world views of non-Western individuals, and respectfully knowing and understanding theory and research from previously 'Other(ed)' perspectives (Battiste, 2000; Datta, 2018; Smith, 2012)" (cited in Thambinathan and Kinsella 2021: 1–2). While emanating from the Indigenous paradigm, the concept of decolonizing research has implications far beyond those communities as, at its core, is a call for anti-oppressive research. We can ask ourselves: How do we confront the "epistemic oppression created by colonial legacies and knowledge systems?" (Thambinathan and Kinsella 2021: 3). As immigrant and refugee populations are present in many research contexts (whether visible or not), how can the legacy of colonialism be resisted through the use of culturally responsive mixed methods research?

Another issue relevant for relationship building in Indigenous communities is that of trust, even when the researcher is from the same community. Pohatu and Warmenhoven (2007) described the challenges they encountered in their work with Māori in New Zealand, even though they were members of this community. One challenge was working within the tensions of different expectations for the research within diverse groups in the community. No community is homogeneous and differences are to be expected in terms of personalities, goals, and access to resources. Pohatu and Warmenhoven worked with the formal structures in the Māori community to validate the participatory nature of the research and to demonstrate values of taking responsibility and planning for mutual benefit.

Recall that one of the strategies that is prioritized in Indigenous research is that of forming relationships. In mixed methods research, the forming of relationships is complex and includes how to respectfully form relationships not only with communities, but also across disciplines. The challenges associated with building relationships in mixed methods studies are addressed in the next section.

Creating Effective Relationships in Mixed Methods: Inclusion of Community Voices

Historically, community-based participatory research (CBPR) has provided a model for inclusion of community voices. However, the combination of CBPR and mixed methods is more nascent and provides opportunities and challenges (DeJonckheere, Lindquist-Grantz, Toraman, Haddad, and Vaughn 2019). CBPR is characterized as a method that incorporates community members as co-researchers in equitable partnerships with opportunities for capacity building and action based on research for community improvements. DeJonckheere et al. (2019) conducted a literature review of studies that included both CBPR and mixed methods. They found that mixed methods provided an opportunity to increase the impact of their studies, foster participation and collaboration, and build interventions that were more responsive to community needs. A challenge in combining these two approaches is in the construction and maintenance of an equitable partnership throughout the research. How can mixed methods be used to assess community strengths, identify community priorities, conduct research that benefits the community, share and use findings, and sustain the partnerships? Mixed methods researchers could hold up a mirror to their practice and collect data testing their assumption that combining CBPR and mixed methods does result in improved rigor, relevance, and impact of their studies.

Forming relationships across cultures is another challenge that is present in mixed methods studies (and all studies in multi-cultural contexts). Harris (2021) addressed this issue in the context of studies conducted in international development in two regions: the Caribbean and Africa. Mixed methods in international development provides an opportunity and a challenge to explore how culture and logistics influence methodological choices. Many of the constructs used in research are defined differently in different cultures. Using mixed methods to explore the meaning of constructs within a culture can avoid making assumptions that the construct has the same meaning to the community compared to what was intended by the researcher. A contextual analysis can reveal the impact of historical and cultural factors on the understanding of a concept. For example, the concept of acceptable risk can be influenced by a collapse of the economic sector, sustained conflict, government corruption, or an epidemic. Gathering data about these contextual and historical factors can then help in the design of data collection strategies that are more informed by local conditions. The use of a Made in Africa or Indigenous Caribbean lens in such studies is in early stages of development. This is a challenge for mixed methods researchers, especially those who work in international development (Chilisa 2020; Chilisa and Mertens 2021; Mertens 2020b).

Working with communities sounds like such a good idea, but in practice, many challenges can arise. This was the case in a study that was described in Chapter 3 by Arko-Achemfuor et al. (2019) about improving life chances for farmers in South Africa. The researchers worked closely with the community members to raise literacy levels and to improve farming practices, only to see their efforts fail several times because of unfulfilled promises from donors, a severe drought, trucks breaking down that were needed to take products to market, and lack of access to financial resources. The researchers realized that their relationship with the community was fragile, so they asked themselves the questions: What to do when the community wants to gives up?

> Some of the farmers were deeply discouraged by these setbacks and some decided to give up. Some members of the community also started to complain to the chief, as they had expected to see their village greening at a rapid pace and jobs being created. They were also frustrated by the fact that many government officials who had visited the hub made empty promises to the farmers and the community at large. To resolve these conflicts, the chief played a major role by mediating and updating the community on progress that had been made, and most importantly, assuring them of BII's [Bokamoso Impact Investments] commitment to the village, despite current challenges. Lesego [the head of BII] considers that it was important to include the chief on any issues encountered with individual community members and farmers. As a result, overall, the community takes pride in the Agri hub.
>
> (Arko-Achemfuor et al. 2019: 3)

The researchers recognized that they could not over-promise results from their work and that the road to success would be challenging. However, they relied on relationships between themselves, the village chief, the investment impact agency, and the farmers to keep communications open. The use of mixed methods to assess the wider context in which interventions occur provides data that can lead to a better understanding of why communities grow frustrated and how to provide the support needed to carry on.

If you are a parent, a teacher, or in any other position to work with youth, you know that there can be challenges in forming relationships that are positive and respectful. This social phenomenon also appears in the research world. Garnett, et al.'s (2019) study used a transformative mixed methods design to address inequities in one school district that was described in Chapter 3. Their work provides insights into the dynamics of building trusting relationships with youth while addressing power inequities. They described the tensions that arose as they moved through the process of establishing relationships with youth who were not immediately inclined to trust adults, and they took deliberate steps to address the issue.

> We are critically conscious of the ways in which our positioning as adults, and predominately white adults, may initially render 'unearned trust' (trust is based on a member's title or role with limited or no direct interaction) but hopefully move towards proxy trust (partners are working together because someone who is trusted invited them) and then ultimately to 'critical reflective trust' (trust that allows for mistakes and where differences can be talked about and resolved) (Lucero et al. 2018: 9).
>
> (cited in Garnett et al. 2019: 8)

Garnett et al. (2019) described the strategies they used to build trust: "experiential learning activities, vocabulary exercises, and story-telling" (9) that were focused on discrimination in the school on the basis of ability, race, religion, and gender. After four weeks of these activities, indicators of trust were recorded in that the middle school students were actively debating the validity of preliminary survey results about perceived discrimination in the school. The students also initiated contact with the adult facilitators about concerns they had about the nature of the research questions. The students' concerns were taken seriously and used to change the research questions and the direction of the intervention. The adults were then able to reflect on the assumptions they had made about the level of trust they had hoped to generate. They modified their own practices to have continuous communications with the students to ensure that student voices were being given priority in the research process. They acknowledged a very real concern of their own: they wanted to avoid taking actions that would violate the trust of the students. They cited Ozer et al. (2013): "A potentially more worrisome byproduct of transformative mixed methods youth participatory action research, is the façade of equity and social justice and the potential for reifying the power of privileged voices and school-based settings that condition 'bounded empowerment' of youth (Ozer et al. 2013)" (cited in Garnett et al. 2019: 9).

Ethics and Mixed Methods

There is some controversy surrounding the idea that there are different ethical issues in mixed methods research as compared with mono-method research. Generally, all researchers, regardless of method, need to be approved through an ethical review process (Mertens 2020a). Plano Clark and Ivankova (2016) endorse the ethical review process for all research and raise ethical issues that might arise in mixed methods research. For example, collecting quantitative data through standardized instruments and qualitative data through open-ended interviews may require additional details about the personal nature of the qualitative data. Informed consent will be more complicated, requiring either two informed consent documents, one for quantitative and one for qualitative, or one more elaborate informed consent document if the same people participate in both aspects of the study. If the same people participate in both parts of the study, then they may be required to reveal more personally identifying information in order to link the two data sets. So, ethical issues do arise about anonymity and time commitment of individuals.

Fetters (2020) also supports the ethical review process as a necessary step in mixed methods research and adds some thoughts about ethical considerations in mixed methods:

Before embarking on a MMR [Mixed Methods Research] study, the investigator should fully consider whether the additional burden on subjects from mixed methods data collection justifies the added value that conducting a mixed methods project will produce. In other words, is the benefit of collecting both types of data, and the associated burden on the subject, justified relative to the incremental burden encompassed by a mixed methods study? Second, when conducting advocacy and participatory studies such as a transformative design, the investigator needs to carefully choose community members who can represent the targeted population.

(161)

Thus, Fetters (2020) raises questions about how ethical issues might differ depending on the paradigmatic framework used in the mixed methods research. The implications of ethical assumptions within each of the paradigmatic frameworks have been integrated throughout this text. For example, researchers in the Constructivist, Transformative, and Indigenous paradigms have placed more importance on the researcher being aware of how their own values, perspectives, and experiences affect the research process (Preissle, Glover-Kudon, Rohan, Boehm, and DeGroff 2015). Constructivists have also been at the forefront of questioning the influence of the researcher's power to develop quantitative data collection tools that might impose culturally reified concepts on a community. Transformative and Indigenous researchers have emphasized the need to provide support for transformative action. This stance is fraught with ethical implications about who can decide what is needed, the importance of researchers not over-promising changes that are determined by factors outside of their control, and the structuring of studies in ways that support sustained changes.

Members of Indigenous communities have, in some parts of the world, developed a code of ethics that is particular to their community. For example, the National Ethics Advisory Committee (2019) developed the *National Ethical Standards for Health and Disability Research and Quality Improvement* with specific guidance for research in the Māori community. The Australian Institute of Aboriginal and Torres Strait Islanders Studies (2020) developed a code of ethics for Aboriginal and Torres Strait Islanders research. Hayward, Sjoblom, Sinclair, and Cidro (2021) reviewed twenty different sets of ethical guidelines for research with Indigenous populations in Canada. Members of the Deaf community have also prepared Terms of Reference for conducting ethical research in the American Sign Language community which have been translated into American Sign Language (Harris, MacGlaughlin, Mertens, and Perez 2020). The purpose here is not to provide details about these ethical protocols. Rather, the purpose is to present the application of ethical protocols for specific communities in mixed methods research, a process that has not yet been undertaken.

The differences in assumptions that characterize the various paradigms raise questions for mixed methods researchers, dependent upon their choice of paradigm. Hesse-Biber (2015b) noted ethical implications about being too prescriptive about mixed methods researchers in complex cultural contexts when mapping out a study:

> Before using any inquiry map, it might be important to ask some questions, such as: Whose viewpoint was taken into account in the mapping process? What does the map exclude? Will following a specific map and its research trails reproduce someone else's reality, research experience, interests, and agenda? Who benefits from following a specific trail or set of trails? What are the ethical conundrums in any mapping design? ... How can we unearth the ethical substructure of the MMMR [Multimethod and Mixed Methods Research] terrain that still remains subjugated?
>
> (Hesse-Biber, 2015b: xlv)

Preissle et al. (2015) note that mixed methods ethical challenges arise around the topics of the inclusion of subjugated voices, examination of outliers that might represent a marginalized portion of the community, and investigation of contradictions that surface from comparisons of quantitative and qualitative results. With cyclical designs (often used in the Transformative paradigm), researchers revise their research plans based on data collected in earlier phases (Mertens 2020a). This raises questions regarding the ethical approval that might have been given to the original plan for research. How do mixed methods researchers, who are critically reflexive, respond when cultural and historical factors indicate the need to change directions? This was seen in the Arko-Achemfuor et al. (2019) study with African farmers and in the Lucero et al. (2018) study in Native American communities. The methods and interventions evolved through the different phases of the study, thus necessitating critical reflection on the ethics of those changes.

Challenging Traditional Methodological Practices to Incorporate Mixed Methods

Plano Clark and Ivankova (2016) recognized the influence of researchers' primary disciplines on their choices with regard to the use of mixed methods.

> Although techniques are not strictly tied to paradigms and methods, the manner in which they are developed, ordered, and otherwise combined can be difficult as researchers with divergent viewing positions and methodological proclivities attempt to work out samples and sampling strategies, data collection tools and procedures, approaches to analyzing quantitative and qualitative data sets, and other shop-floor practices in ways that ensure rigor.
>
> (Hemmings et al. 2013: 262)

Fàbregues, Escalante-Barrios, Molina-Azorin, Hong, and Verd (2021) conducted a mixed methods study to compare experiences with mixed methods in the disciplines of education, nursing, psychology, and sociology. They reported greater concern with issues around philosophical foundations of mixed methods in the sociological community than in the other disciplines.

Hemmings et al. (2013) noted the challenges encountered when medical and social scientists came together for a mixed methods study. One challenge came from the traditional methodologies used in each discipline: "Researchers at the methods level generally gravitate toward methodologies associated with their disciplines such as the tendency of medical researchers to conduct experimental or other types of studies involving quantitative measures and of anthropologists to immerse themselves in ethnographic fieldwork" (2013: 262). The team in this study consisted of two nursing researchers, one steeped in quantitative methods and the other in mixed methods, and two educational researchers, both of who primarily used qualitative methods. The team shared an interest in aspects of organizational culture that contribute to improved health for workers. Initial team meetings revealed a lack of understanding among the team members of their respective assumptions, methods, and ways of working together. The team members shared literature from their own fields and spent time discussing the implications of the readings for working together as a team. Based on additional literature review and discussions, the team worked toward building an interdisciplinary theoretical framework for their mixed methods study. This was a challenging process:

> The process was certainly frustrating for members of the nursing and education team and was exacerbated at times by psychological dissonance emanating from identity conflicts. Some members struggled mightily with their self-concepts as researchers as they ploughed through unfamiliar literature, tried to navigate foreign academic languages and discourses, encountered incomprehensible viewing positions and otherwise experienced tough border crossings that were threatening their sense of competency, or pulling them away from familiar intellectual terrains.
>
> (Hemmings et al. 2013: 266)

Hemmings and colleagues noted that going through this process is very time-consuming and requires additional resources.

Kong et al. (2018) also noted that mixed methods studies require additional time and resources, suggesting this constraint may make the use of mixed methods less feasible for some researchers. In their study on environmental education (described in Chapter 3), Kong and colleagues recognized that extra time and resources would be needed, so they began applying for research grants early in the planning stages.

Increasing the Impact of Mixed Methods Research: Meeting Grand Challenges

Grand challenges, sometimes called wicked problems (Mertens 2015), are problems across the globe that seem to be intransigent where there is no single solution that is agreed to. These include such issues as the climate crisis; the status of refugees and immigrants; increasing gaps in wealth between rich and poor; violence and conflicts; a global pandemic; disparities in economic, educational, and health systems; and violations of the rights of racial and ethnic minorities, women and girls, and people with disabilities. Mixed methods researchers are at a point where they can ask themselves: What is our role in addressing these grand challenges? What can we as a community do to increase social, economic, and environmental justice? Is this an appropriate role for researchers?

While the transformative and Indigenous approaches to mixed methods center these questions, the good news is that mixed methods research across the board can make a choice to contribute to improving justice. The sample studies presented in Chapter 3 provide examples of mixed methods researchers tackling these grand challenges in all the paradigms. Post-positivist mixed methods researchers addressed the issue of environmental education (Kong et al. 2018) and prevention of intimate partner violence (Rees-Evan and Pevalin 2017). Constructivists examined ways to support people living with dementia (Harding et al. 2021). Pragmatic mixed methods researchers studied how to respond to food emergencies (Shannon et al. 2021) and to provide better health care for persons with chronic health conditions (Holtrop et al. 2019). Transformative mixed methods researchers supported changes to address discrimination in schools (Garnett et al. 2019) and health care for members of threatened sexual minority groups (Miller 2020). Indigenous mixed methods researchers developed interventions to improve the lives of farmers in poor communities (Arko-Achemfuor et al. 2019) and to reduce health disparities in Indigenous communities (Lucero et al. 2018).

Tremendous challenges and opportunities are present for researchers whose philosophical assumptions support their engagement in pursuing solutions to grand challenges and increasing justice. I argue that the impact of mixed methods research can be stronger when researchers use thoughtful designs that explicitly address issues of discrimination and oppression. When members of marginalized and vulnerable communities, along with persons in formal positions of power, are respectfully included in the research planning, implementation, and use, then there is a great probability that the results will be used for transformative purposes.

Researchers and the communities they serve can increase the potential for transformative change by incorporating lessons learned from social activism and social change agents. This might be considered to be a controversial position given that other research frameworks call for a separation between research and advocacy. However, continuing to do research in a business-as-usual manner puts the researcher in the unethical position of being complicit in sustaining oppression. By adopting the role of change agent, researchers have the opportunity to disrupt that historical legacy and contribute to a transformed world (Hall 2020).

(cited in Mertens in press)

Challenges come with adopting what some would consider to be a controversial stance on the role of researchers. However, separating the role of researcher from social activist may leave researchers complicit in supporting an oppressive status quo. One of the challenges rests in the culture of the research community. Other challenges surface in methodological terms: Just how are researchers supposed to design their studies to support increased justice? Researchers may not have training or experience in incorporating the strengths of community members and integrating their knowledge, skills, and experience into the planning, implementation, and use of research. Researchers might be uncomfortable raising questions about the historical and structural inequities that continue to subjugate members of marginalized communities.

Chouinard and Cram (2021) argue that, when working with communities who have been historically marginalized, the intersection of ethics, values, and culture is essential. Researchers work from professional standards and principles; however, these have not proven to be sufficient to change an oppressive status quo. Attention needs to be paid to relationship building that explicitly addresses disparities of power and privilege and challenges values and worldviews that are not supportive of the changes communities need. Opening up discussion of these issues provides one pathway to decolonizing methodologies and practices. There is a need to "interrogate the responsibility of [researchers] to support a viable future for our planet, including working to ensure good relations between generations to come and the environments needed to nurture and sustain them (Kimmerer 2013)" (cited in Chouinard and Cram 2021: 237).

The climate crisis affects everyone across the globe, threatening well-being because of health problems, destruction of property, and economic repercussions. Hence, tackling environmental problems is a grand challenge. Ida Widianingsih, vice-dean for Learning,

Research, and Student Affairs at UnPad in Indonesia, addressed the challenge by recruiting students into a course that was designed to be interdisciplinary, focused on ecological issues, and an opportunity to contribute to increased justice in one village in Indonesia (Interview conducted by Donna Mertens, October 2021). The class members gathered data about the economic, health, and environmental impact of villagers losing their land who then moved to the river bank, endangering the health of the river. Ida contacted the Head of the village and government officials to identify land that was owned by the Ministry of Forestry and the private company that had started a tea plantation almost 100 years ago. The students who came from urban planning are designing a low-income housing project for the land that the company was not currently using for tea cultivation. This is an ongoing project, so they have to see what will happen. The students are using a transformative mixed methods lens to base their understanding of the context on quantitative and qualitative data and to design a housing plan that will provide housing for the landless and protect the river. They plan to collect both quantitative and qualitative data to document the process and outcomes of this project. They will use technology to collect and communicate their work through Instagram, videos, podcasts, mapping, and comics. Widianingsih commented:

> I want to continue my impact no matter how small. Because who knows, some of my students may continue my ideas. Most of the students join me because they have to do a practical course, but I believe some of them in the future will continue the ideas. I just want to do something that brings change to the community. I think transformative research needs to be understood not as just academic. We have to leave our traditional research that is just theoretical. When we support transformative research, we can have hope for the future.
> (Interview conducted by Donna Mertens, October 2021)

Dencer-Brown, Jarvis, Allfaro, and Milne (2021) used a social-ecological framework in a mixed methods study to investigate the relationship between humans and the natural world as a means to enhancing environmental management in New Zealand. Removal and expansion of mangroves along coastal areas is related to changes in biodiversity and is a polarizing issue for the people who live along the coast. The researchers knew that issues of cultural context were important and that inherent power dynamics meant they needed to be inclusive of scientists, decision makers, and community members. Initially, the researchers thought the study would be purely exploratory; however, their interactions with a broad range of stakeholders led them to see this as a way to catalyze action on the management of this ecosystem with community input. Traditional interviewing methods were used with the management staff at the removal sites. However, the researchers were guided by Indigenous residents in obtaining information from their communities. This meant that the researchers set up meetings to introduce themselves to Māori leaders and community members; interviews were conducted more as conversations; and the focus was on their vision of a healthy harbor and the presence of the mangroves.

The information was shared through local and regional councils, government offices, independent ecologists, conservation groups, and the participants who were interviewed (Dencer-Brown et al. 2021). The intent of the information sharing was to inform community members who were lodging appeals to remove mangroves about the trade-offs in terms of damage to the ecosystem. While the study came to an end, a sustainable future depends on continuous engagement with local communities, ongoing monitoring of ecological status, and working with individuals with competing interests. Mixed methods researchers face challenges in incorporating an increase in environmental justice in their work.

In 2019, the world saw the beginning of a pandemic of the coronavirus that was highly contagious and often lethal. The spread of this virus has been difficult to contain and has upended the social and economic lives of the world's citizens. It has also laid bare the inequities in the health, education, and economic systems worldwide as data emerges on who is getting sick and dying, who is getting vaccinated, who is losing jobs, who is benefiting economically as the pandemic continues, and who is experiencing a disruption in education (Büyüm, Kenney, Koris, Mkumba, and Raveendran 2020). Fetters and Molina-Azorin (2021a) noted the impact on researchers during this time of catastrophic changes:

Routines for conducting research changed dramatically. In-person data collection of many sorts were put on hold. Many research offices, laboratories, and centers were closed. Observations of actual behaviors became limited. Human subjects reviews were postponed, and the types of research approved highly restricted. Researchers returned funds to funding agencies as they were unable to conduct studies. As much of social interaction moved into the virtual space, researchers who were able, moved much of their research online. Interviews when they have occurred, have often moved online. Researchers have rediscovered or changed their projects to use secondary datasets.

(Fetters and Molina-Azorin 2021: 296)

They called upon mixed methods researchers to share the innovations in methodologies that they developed in response to these challenges. In response to this call, they published a special issue of the *Journal of Mixed Methods Research* with articles that not only described innovative methodological features, but also demonstrated socially engaged research to solve societal problems and promote a better world. In this special issue, Riha, Abreu Lopes, Ibrahim, and Srinivasan (2021) described a mixed methods approach in Somalia that involved using interactive radio-short message service (SMS) that had been used previously during a cholera outbreak in 2017. They drew parallels to its use in the context of Covid-19 epidemic, especially in low- and middle-income countries where access to technology is limited, but radio and mobile phones are more accessible. They used this method to collect both quantitative and qualitative data from radio audiences, analyzed the qualitative data for themes, then quantitized the qualitative data, and explored statistical associations between the emergent themes and demographic variables. Through this method, they were able to gather information about the perceived risks of contracting cholera, what could be done to improve water quality, and the trustworthy sources of information about cholera. The participants provided their responses following radio shows that asked them to share their viewpoints. The advantages of this approach were the ability to connect with people who might have been hard to reach otherwise, the use of local languages, and rapid production of information needed in a health crisis. The disadvantage is that the sample is self-selecting and the responses to questions are relatively short because of the medium used to collect the data. Researchers face challenges in contexts of economic adversity, especially when there is health crisis.

Ho, Chen, Shao, Bao, Ai, Tarfa, Brossard, Brown, and Brauer (2021) used mixed methods to explore the effectiveness of public health messaging as a deterrent to contracting Covid-19 in the United States. The data collection was accomplished through an online survey that had both open and closed-ended questions. The researchers focused on a group that reported that they were not practicing social distancing, a strategy the World Health Organization recommended as a way to avoid infection. The survey also included an open-ended question that asked what kind of message would be persuasive to them to practice more social distancing. The qualitative responses of this subgroup were analyzed using standard qualitative data analysis techniques to identify emergent themes. The researchers then used structural topic modeling to quantitatively analyze the qualitative data. This method counts frequency of phrases and also identifies key words and text content that were associated with the themes. It also allows for comparisons of groups on these themes based on demographic variables such as gender and race. Through this process, the researchers identified ten key topics that revealed which persuasive messages would be effective enough to persuade the participants to engage in social distancing. This research can be used to tailor public health messaging to be more persuasive during a health crisis. Changing people's behavior on a societal level is a big challenge that mixed methods researchers can continue to explore.

Summary

As researchers have consciously focused their attention on how to improve the use of mixed methods relatively recently, many challenges remain. These provide opportunities for those new to mixed methods as well as experienced researchers to contribute to the development of the field. Some of these challenges include: the role of paradigms in mixed methods research and the permeability of borders; incorporation of the Indigenous philosophical paradigm and mixed methods; creating effective relationships in mixed methods and inclusion of community voices; ethics and mixed methods; challenging traditional methodological practices to incorporate mixed methods; and increasing the impact of mixed methods research to meet grand challenges of social, economic, and environmental justice in order to be part of the solution for such societal challenges as the climate crisis; disparities in the economic, educational, and health systems; global and regional conflicts; and pandemics.

Divergent thinking is needed to address these challenges. Fàbregues, Escalante-Barrios, Molina-Azorin, Hong, and Verd's (2021) study about the use of mixed methods revealed a concern on the part of the mixed methods research community about trying to delineate specific typologies and homogenizing terminology and procedures. They fear that such action would negate the true value of using mixed methods. "This attitude towards homogenization of mixed methods research could hinder the advancement of the field since it promotes a uniform approach, suppresses intellectual disputes and ignores the diversity of approaches and attitudes regarding mixed methods found in the literature" (13).

As researchers continue their discussions of methods in terms of qualitative, quantitative, and mixed methods, they are challenged to attend to the larger picture based on contextual and cultural issues that need to be addressed to increase the impact of research in addressing inequities and increasing justice. As exemplified in the studies discussed in this book, integrating strategies of social activists, shifting the role of researcher to social change agent, culturally responsive inclusion of members of marginalized and vulnerable populations, formation of collaboratives or coalitions, explicitly addressing power differences, and planning for sustainability are not unproblematic. However, communities have the strength to guide researchers in ways to overcome these challenges. Researchers can support transformative change by asking themselves, what is the impact of my work? Is it contributing to increased justice or supporting oppression? If researchers make a commitment to increasing justice, then their final question asks: What do I need to do in the design of my research to support transformative change and sustainable impact? (Mertens 2021).

Questions for Further Thinking:

1. What are your thoughts on the role of paradigms in mixed methods research?
2. What aspects of the Indigenous paradigm would add value to your mixed methods research approach?
3. How would you advocate for the use of mixed methods in your discipline?
4. How would you construct a research team in your research area?
5. How can we as a community of mixed methods researchers increase the impact of our work toward improved social, economic, and environmental justice?

FURTHER READINGS AND RESOURCES

Chilisa, B. (2020), *Indigenous Research Methodologies*, Thousand Oaks, CA: Sage.

Fetters, M. D. (2020), *The Mixed Methods Research Workbook*, Thousand Oaks, CA: Sage.

Journal of Mixed Methods Research. (2021), Aims and Scope. Accessed July 27, 2021. https://journals.sagepub.com/aims-scope/MMR

Mason, J. (2006), "Six strategies for mixing methods and lining data in social science research." Economic & Social Research Council National Centre for Research Methods. Working Paper Series. https://eprints.ncrm.ac.uk/id/eprint/482/1/0406_six%2520strategies%2520for%2520mixing%2520methods.pdf

Maxwell, J. A. (2016), "Expanding the history and range of mixed methods research," *Journal of Mixed Methods Research*, 10(1): 12–27.

Mertens, D. M. (2018), *Mixed Methods Design in Evaluation*, Thousand Oaks, CA: Sage.

Mertens, D. M. (2020a), *Research and Evaluation in Education and Psychology*, 5th ed., Thousand Oaks, CA: Sage.

Mertens, D. M. and A. T. Wilson (2019), *Program Evaluation Theory and Practice*, 2nd ed., New York: Guilford Press.

Mixed Methods International Research Association. https://mmira.wildapricot.org/

Transformative research and evaluation. https://transformativeresearchandevaluation.com

REFERENCES

Arko-Achemfuor, A. and D. Y. Dzansi (2015), "Business doing well by doing good in the community," *The Journal of Commerce*, 7(2): 53–68.

Arko-Achemfuor, A., N. Romm and L. Serolong (2019), "Academic-practitioner collaboration with communities towards social and ecological transformation," *International Journal for Transformative Research*, 6(10): 1–9.

Australian Institute of Aboriginal and Torres Strait Islanders Studies (2020), "AIATSIS code of ethics for Aboriginal and Torres Strait Islander research," in *Canberra*, Australia: Australian Institute of Aboriginal and Torres Strait Islander Studies. Accessed October 11, 2021. https://aiatsis.gov.au/sites/default/files/2020-10/aiatsis-code-ethics.pdf

Babbie, E. R. (1992), *The Practice of Social Research*, Belmont, CA: Wadsworth.

Bamberger, M. V. Rao and M. Woolcock (2010), *Using Mixed Methods in Monitoring and Evaluation: Experiences from International Development*, Washington, DC: The World Bank.

Barnes, T. J. (2008), "American pragmatism: Towards a geographical introduction," *Geoforum*, 39(4): 1542–54.

Battiste, M. A. (2000), *Reclaiming Indigenous Voice and Vision*, British Columbia, Canada: UBC Press.

Bazeley, P. (2018), *Integrating Analysis in Mixed Methods Research*, London: SAGE Publications.

Bird-Naytowhow, K., A. R. Hatala, T. Pearl, A. Judge and E. Sjoblom (2017), "Ceremonies of relationship: Engaging urban Indigenous youth in community-based research," *International Journal of Qualitative Methods*, 16: 1–14. DOI: 10.1177/1609406917707899

Bogaert, I., K. De Marelaer, B. Deforche, P. Clarys, and E. Zinzen (2015), "The physically active lifestyle of Flemish secondary school teachers: A mixed-methods approach towards developing a physical activity intervention," *Health Education Journal*, 74(3): 326–39.

Bhuyan, M. R. and Y. Zhang (2020), "A mixed methods research strategy to study children's play and urban physical environment in Dhaka," *Journal of Mixed Methods Research*, 14(3): 358–78.

Brannen, J. (Ed.) (1992), *Mixing Methods: Qualitative and Quantitative Research*, New York, NY: Routledge. DOI: https://doi.org/10.4324/9781315248813

Bryman, A. (1988), *Quantity and Quality in Social Research*, New York, NY: Routledge.

Buri, J. R. (1991), "Parental authority questionnaire," *Journal of Personality Assessment*, 57: 110–19.

Büyüm, A. M., C. Kenney, A. Koris, L. Mkumba and Y. Raveendran (2020), "Decolonising global health: If not now, when?" *British Medical Journal Global Health*, e003394. DOI: 10.1136/bmjgh-2020-003394

Campbell, D. T. and D. W. Fiske (1956), "Convergent and discriminant validation by multitrait multidimensional matrix," *Psychological Bulletin*, 56: 81–105.

Chilisa, B. (2020), *Indigenous Research Methodologies*, Thousand Oaks, CA: Sage.

Chilisa, B. and D. M. Mertens (2021), "Indigenous Made in Africa evaluation frameworks: Addressing epistemic violence and contributing to social transformation," *American Journal of Evaluation*, 42(2): 241–53. DOI: 10.1177/1098214020948601

Cheek, J., D. L. Lipschitz, E. M. Abrams, D. R. Vago and Y. Nakamura (2015), "Dynamic reflexivity in action: An armchair walk through of a qualitatively driven mixed-methods and multiple methods study of mindfulness training in schoolchildren," *Qualitative Health Research*, 25(6): 751–62.

Claasen, N., N. M. Covic, E. F. Idsardi, L. A. Sandham, A. Gildenhuys and S. Lemke (2015), "Applying a transdisciplinary mixed methods research design to explore sustainable diets in South Africa," *International Journal of Qualitative Methods*, 14(2): 69–91. DOI: 10.1177/160940691501400207

Chouinard, J. A. and F. Cram (2020), *Culturally Responsive Approaches to Evaluation*, Thousand Oaks, CA: Sage.

Chouinard, J. A. and F. Cram (2021), "Introduction to the ethics, values and culture section," *American Journal of Evaluation*, 42(2): 237–40.

Colditz, J. B., J. Welling, N. A. Smith, A. E. James and B. A. Primack (2019), "World Vaping day: Contextualizing Vaping culture in online social media using a mixed methods approach," *Journal of Mixed Methods Research*, 13(2): 196–215. DOI: 10.1177/1558689817702753

Cram, F. (2016), "Lessons on decolonizing evaluation from Kaupapa Maori evaluation," *Canadian Journal of Program Evaluation*, 30(3): 296–312.

Cram, F., B. Chilisa and D.M. Mertens (2013), "The journey begins", in D.M. Mertens, F. Cram, and B. Chilisa (Eds.), *Indigenous Pathways into Social Research*, 11-40, Walnut Creek, CA: Left Coast Press.

Cram, F. and D. M. Mertens (2015), "Transformative and indigenous frameworks for multimethod and mixed methods research," in S. Hesse-Biber and R. B. Johnson (Eds.), *The Oxford Handbook of Multimethod and Mixed Methods Research Inquiry*, 91–109, Oxford: Oxford Press.

Creswell, J. and V. Plano Clark (2011), *Designing and Conducting Mixed Methods Research*, 2nd ed., Thousand Oaks, CA: Sage.

Creswell, J. W., A. C. Klassen, V. Plano Clark and K. C. Smith (2020), *Best Practices for Mixed Methods Research in the Health Sciences*, Washington, DC: National Institutes of Health Office of Behavioral and Social Sciences Research.

Cronenberg, S. (2020), "Paradigm parley: A framework for the dialectical stance," *Journal of Mixed Methods Research*, 14(1): 26–46.

Curry, L. A., A. O'Cathain, V. L. Plano Clark, R. Aroni, M. Fetters and D. Berg (2012), "The role of group dynamics in mixed methods health sciences research teams," *Journal of Mixed Methods Research*, 6(1): 5–20.

Datta, R. (2018), "Decolonizing both researcher and research and its effectiveness in Indigenous research," *Research Ethics*, 14(2): 1–24. DOI: https://doi.org/10.1177/1747016117733296

DeJonckheere, R., S. T. Lindquist-Grantz, K. Haddad and L. M. Vaughn (2019), "Intersection of mixed methods and community-based participatory research: A methodological review," *Journal of Mixed Methods Research*, 13(4): 481–502.

Dencer-Brown, A. M., R. M. Jarvis, A. C. Alfaro and S. Milne (2021), "The mixed methods practical sustainability research framework: An illustration from research on the creeping problem of coastal complexity and mangrove management," *Journal of Mixed Methods Research*. DOI: 10.1177/15586898211014422

Denzin, N. (2012), "Triangulation 2.0," *Journal of Mixed Methods Research*, 6(2): 80–8.

Du Bois, W. E. B. (1899), *The Philadelphia Negro*, Philadelphia: University of Pennsylvania Press.

Edwards, R., H. M. Barnes, D. McGregor and T. Brannelly (2020), "Supporting indigenous and non-indigenous research partnerships," *The Qualitative Report*, 25(13): 6–15. https://nsuworks.nova.edu/tqr/vol25/iss13/2

Fàbregues, S., E. L. Escalante-Barrios, J. F. Molina-Azorin, Q. N. Hong and J. M. Verd (2021), "Taking a critical stance towards mixed methods research: A cross-disciplinary qualitative secondary analysis of researchers' views," *PLoS ONE*, 16(7): e0252014. DOI: https://doi.org/10.1371/journal.pone.0252014

Feilzer, M. (2009), "Doing mixed methods research pragmatically: Implications for the rediscovery of pragmatism as a research paradigm," *Journal of Mixed Methods Research*, 4(1): 6–16.

Fetters, M. D. (2016), "'Haven't we always been doing mixed methods research?': Lessons learned from the development of the horseless carriage," *Journal of Mixed Methods Research*, 10(1): 3–11.

Fetters, M. D. (2020), *The Mixed Methods Research Workbook*, Thousand Oaks, CA: Sage.

Fetters, M. and J. F. Molina-Azorin (2021a), "Special issue on COVID-19 and novel mixed methods methodological approaches during catastrophic social change," *Journal of Mixed Methods Research*, 15(3): 295–303.

Fetters, M. and J. F. Molina-Azorin (2021b), "Guidance on using mixed methods from diverse international organizations in the behavioral, social, fundamental, and health sciences," *Journal of Mixed Methods Research*, 15(4): 470–84.

Food Risc Resource Centre (2016), "Mixed methods research What is it?" Dublin Ireland. Accessed October 29, 2021. http://resourcecentre. foodrisc.org/mixed-methods-research_185.html

Garnett, B. R., L. C. Smith, C. T. Kervick, T. A. Ballysingh, M. Moore and E. Gonell (2019), "The emancipatory potential of transformative mixed methods designs: Informing youth participatory action research and restorative practices within a district-wide school transformation project," *International Journal of Research & Method in Education*. DOI: 10.1080/1743727X.2019.1598355

Gibbs, A., L. Washington, S. Willan, N. Ntini, T. Khumalo, N. Mbatha, Y. Sikweyiya, N. Shai, E. Chirwa, M. Strauss, G. Ferrari and R. Jewkes (2017), "The Stepping stones and creating futures intervention to prevent intimate partner violence and HIV-risk behaviors in Durban South Africa: Study protocol for a cluster randomized control trial, and baseline characteristics," *BMC Public Health*, 17: 336–51. DOI: 10.1186/s12889-017-4223-x

Glaser, B. G. and A. L. Strauss (1967), *The Discovery of Grounded Theory: Strategies for Qualitative Research*, Chicago, IL: Aldine.

Greene, J. and J. N. Hall (2010), "Dialectics and pragmatism: Being of consequence," in A. Tashakkori and C. Teddlie (Eds.), *SAGE Handbook of Mixed Methods Research in Social and Behavioral Research*, 2nd ed., 119–43, Thousand Oaks, CA: Sage.

Greene, J. C. and V. J. Caracelli (1997), "Defining and describing the paradigm issue in mixed-methods evaluation," *New Directions for Evaluation*, 74: 5–17. DOI: 10.1002/ev.1068

Guba, E. and Y. Lincoln (1989), *Fourth Generation Evaluation*, Thousand Oaks, CA: Sage.

Guba, E. and Y.S. Lincoln (2005), "Paradigmatic controversies, contradictions, and emerging confluences," in N.K. Denzin and

Y.S. Lincoln (Eds.), *Handbook of Qualitative Research*, 191–216, Thousand Oaks, CA: Sage.

Guetterman, T. C., J. W. Creswell, C. Deutsch and J. J. Gallo (2019), "Process evaluation of a retreat for scholars in the first cohort: The NIH mixed methods research training program for the health sciences," *Journal of Mixed Methods Research*, 13(1): 52–68.

Hall, J. (2013), "Pragmatism, evidence, and mixed methods evaluation," in D. M. Mertens and S. Hesse Biber (Eds.), *Mixed Methods and Credibility of Evidence in Evaluation, New Directions for Evaluation*, 138, 15–26.

Hall, M.E. (2020), "Blest be the tie that binds", in L.C. Newbauer, D. McBride, A.D. Guajardo, W.D. Casillas and M.E. Hall (Eds.), *Examining Issues Facing Communities of Color Today: The Role of Evaluation to Incite Change, New Directions for Evaluation*, 166: 13–22.

Harding, E., M. P. Sullivan, K. S. X. Yong and S. J. Crutch (2021), "Into the ordinary: Lessons learned from a mixed-methods study in the homes of people living with dementia," in P. M. Camic (Ed.), *Qualitative Research in Psychology: Expanding Perspectives in Methodology and Design*, 2nd ed, 235–62, Washington, DC: American Psychological Association.

Harney, L., J. McCurry, J. Scott and J. Wills (2016), "Developing 'process pragmatism' to underpin engaged research in human geography," *Progress in Human Geography*, 40(3): 316–33.

Harris, J. (2021), "Mixed methods research in developing country contexts: Lessons from field research in six countries across Africa and the Caribbean," *Journal of Mixed Methods Research*, 1–18. DOI: 10.1177/15586898211032825

Harris, R., H. MacGlaughlin, D. M. Mertens and J. Perez (2020), "Research ethics for sign language communities [ASL Translation]," *Deaf Studies Digital Journal* volume 5.

Hayward, A., E. Sjoblom, S. Sinclair and J. Cidro (2021), "A new era of Indigenous research: Community-based Indigenous research ethics protocols in Canada," *Journal of Empirical Research on Human Research Ethics*: 1–15. DOI: 10.1177/15562646211023705

Hemmings, A., G. Beckett, S. Kennerly and T. Yap (2013), "Building a community of research practice: Intragroup team social dynamics in interdisciplinary mixed methods," *Journal of Mixed Methods Research*, 7(3): 261–73.

Henwood, W. and R. Henwood (2011), "Mana Whenua Kaitiakitanga in action: Restoring the Mauri of Lake Ōmāpere," *AlterNative: An International Journal of Indigenous Peoples*, 7(3): 220–32. DOI: 10.1177/117718011100700303

Hesse Biber, S. (2010), *Mixed Methods Research*, New York: Guilford Press.

Hesse-Biber, S. N. (2015a), "Mixed methods research: The 'thing-ness' problem," *Qualitative Health Research*, 25(6): 775–88.

Hesse-Biber, S. (2016), "Doing interdisciplinary mixed methods health care research: Working the boundaries, tensions, and synergistic potential of team-based research," *Qualitative Health Research*, 26(5): 649–58. DOI: https://doi.org/10.1177/1049732316634304

Hesse-Biber, S. (2015b), "Introduction: Navigating a turbulent research landscape: Working the boundaries, tensions, diversity and contradictions of multimethod and mixed methods Inquiry," in S. Hesse-Biber and R. B. Johnson (Eds.), *The Oxford Handbook of Multimethod and Mixed Methods Research Inquiry*, xxxiii–liii, Oxford, UK: Oxford University Press.

Hesse-Biber, S., D. Rodriguez and N. A. Frost (2015), "A qualitatively drive approach to multimethod and mixed methods research," in S. Hesse-Biber and R. B. Johnson (Eds.), *The Oxford Handbook of Multimethod and Mixed Methods Research Inquiry*, 3–20, Oxford, UK: Oxford University Press.

Ho, P., K. Chen, A. Shao, L. Bao, A. Ai, A. Tarfa, D. Brossard, L. Brown and M. Brauer (2021), "A mixed methods study of public perception of social distancing: Integrating qualitative and computational analyses for text data," *Journal of Mixed Methods Research*, 15(3): 374–97. DOI: doi.org/10.1177/15586898211020862

Hock, E., M. Eberly, S. Bartle-Haring, P. Ellwanger and K. Widaman (2001), "Separation anxiety in parents of adolescents: Theoretical significance and scale development," *Child Development*, 72: 284–98.

Holtrop, J. S., G. Potworowski, L. A. Green and M. Fetters (2019), "Analysis of novel care management programs in primary care: An example of mixed methods in health services research," *Journal of Mixed Methods Research*, 13(1): 85–112.

Howe, K. R. (2004), "A critique of experimentalism," *Qualitative Inquiry*, 10(1): 42–61.

Johnson, R. B. (2012), "Guest editor's editorial: Dialectical pluralism and mixed research," *American Behavioral Scientist*, 56: 751–4.

Johnson, R. B. (2015), "Conclusions: Toward an inclusive and defensible multimethod and mixed methods science," in S. N. Hesse-Biber and R. B. Johnson (Eds.), *The Oxford Handbook of Multimethod and Mixed Methods Research Inquiry*, 688–706, New York: Oxford University Press.

Johnson, R. B., T. Onwuegbuzie and L. A. Turner (2007), "Toward a definition of mixed methods research," *Journal of Mixed Methods Research*, 1(2): 112–33.

Johnson, R. B. and J. Schoonenboom (2015), "Adding qualitative and mixed methods research to health intervention studies: Interacting with differences," *Qualitative Health Research*, 26(5): 587–602. DOI: 10.1177/1049732315617479

Johnson, R. B. and T. Stefurak (2013), "Considering the evidence-and-credibility discussion in evaluation through the lens of dialectical pluralism," in D. M. Mertens and S. Hesse Biber (Eds.), *Mixed Methods and Credibility of Evidence in Evaluation. New Directions in Evaluation*, 138, 37–48.

Journal of Mixed Methods Research (2021), Aims and Scope. Accessed July 27, 2021. https://journals.sagepub.com/aims-scope/MMR

Kacperski, C., R. Ulloa and C. Hall (2019), "Do athletes imagine being the best, or crossing the finish line first? A mixed methods analysis of construal levels in elite athletes' spontaneous imagery," *Journal of Mixed Methods Research*, 13(2): 216–41. DOI: 10.1177/1558689816674563

Khadaroo, A. and F. MacCallum (2021), "Parenting of adolescent single children: A mixed methods study," *Journal of Family Issues*: 1–24. DOI: 10.1177/0192513X21993180

Kimmerer, R. W. (2013), *Braiding Sweetgrass: Indigenous Wisdom, Scientific Knowledge and the Teachings of Plants*, Minneapolis, MN: Milkweed Editions.

Kong, S. Y., N. M. Yaacob and A. R. M. Ariffin (2018), "Constructing a mixed methods research design: Exploration of an architectural intervention," *Journal of Mixed Methods Research*, 12(2): 148–65.

Le Play, F. (1855), *European Workers*, Tours, France: Alfred Mame.

Leal, I., J. Engebretson, L. Cohen, M. E. Fernandez-Esquer, G. Lopez, T. Wangyal and A. Chaoul (2018), "An exploration of the effects of Tibetan yoga on patients' psychological well-being and experience of lymphoma: An experimental embedded mixed methods study," *Journal of Mixed Methods Research*, 12(1): 31–54.

Levitt, H. M., M. Bamberg, J. W. Creswell, D. M. Frost, R. Josselson and C. Suarez-Orozco (2018), "Journal article reporting standards for qualitative primary, qualitative meta-analytic, and mixed methods research in psychology: The APA publications and communications board task force report," *The American Psychologist*, 73: 26–46.

Lucero, J., N. Wallerstein, B. Duran, M. Alegria, E. Greene-Moton, B. Israel, S. Kastelic, M. Magarati, J. Oetzel, C. Pearson, A. Schulz, M. Villegas and E. R. White Hat (2018), "Development of mixed methods investigation of process and outcomes of community-based participatory research," *Journal of Mixed Methods Research*, 12(1): 55–74.

Mason, J. (2006), "Six strategies for mixing methods and lining data in social science research," Economic & Social Research Council National Centre for Research Methods. Working Paper Series. https://eprints.ncrm.ac.uk/id/eprint/482/1/0406_six%2520strategies%2520for%2520mixing%2520methods.pdf

Maxwell, J. A. (2004), "Using qualitative methods for causal explanation," *Field Methods*, 16: 243–64.

Maxwell, J. A. (2016), "Expanding the history and range of mixed methods research," *Journal of Mixed Methods Research*, 10(1): 12–27.

McBride, D., W. Casillas and J. LoPiccolo (2020), "Inciting social change through evaluation," in L. C. Neubauer, D. McBride, A. D. Guajardo, W. D. Casillas and M. E. Hall (Eds.), *Examining Issues Facing Communities of Color Today: The Role of Evaluation to Incite Change. New Directions for Evaluation*, 166, 119–27.

McIntyre-Mills, J., J. Karel, A. Arko-Achemfuor, N. R. A. Romm and L. Serolong (2019), "Efforts to inspire transformative research with farmers in a small town in the North West Province of South Africa," *International Journal for Transformative Research*, 6(10): 10–19.

Menon, S. and J. Hartz-Karp (2020), "Applying mixed methods action research to explore how public participation in an Indian City could better resolve urban sustainability problems," *Action Research*, 0(0): 1–24. DOI: doi.org/10.1177/1476750320943662

Mertens, D. (2010), "Philosophy in mixed methods teaching: The transformative paradigm as illustration," *International Journal of Multiple Research Approaches*, 4: 9–18.

Mertens, D. M. (2014), "A momentous development in mixed methods research," *Journal of Mixed Methods Research*, 8(1): 1–3.

Mertens, D. M. (2015), "Mixed methods and wicked problems," *Journal of Mixed Methods Research*, 9(1): 3–6. DOI: https://doi.org/10.1177/1558689814562944

Mertens, D. M. (2017), "Transformative research: Personal and societal," *International Journal for Transformative Research*, 4(1): 18–24.

Mertens, D. M. (2018), *Mixed Methods Design in Evaluation*, Thousand Oaks, CA: Sage.

Mertens, D. M. (2020a), *Research and Evaluation in Education and Psychology*, 5th ed., Thousand Oaks, CA: Sage.

Mertens, D. M. (2020b), "Transformation as a goal of mixed methods research in the Caribbean," *Caribbean Journal of Mixed Methods Research*, 1(1): 16–28.

Mertens, D. M. (2021), "Transformative research methods to increase social impact for vulnerable groups and cultural minorities," *International Journal of Qualitative Methods*, 20: 1–9.

Mertens, D. M., P. Bazeley, L. Bowleg, N. Fielding, J. Maxwell, J. F. Molina-Azorin and K. Niglas (2016), "Expanding thinking through a kaleidoscopic look into the future: Implications of the Mixed Methods International Research Association's Task Force Report on the Future of Mixed Methods," *Journal of Mixed Methods Research*, 10(3): 221–7.

Mertens, D.M. and T. T. Catsambas (2022), "Practice through a transformative lens and methodological implications in evaluation," in R. D. van den Berg, P. Hawkins and N. Stame, (Eds.), *Ethics for Evaluation: Beyond "doing no harm" to "tackling bad" and "doing good"*, 165–87, London: Routledge.

Mertens, D. M. and F. Cram (2016), "Integration tensions and possibilities: Indigenous research and social transformation," *International Review of Qualitative Research*, 9(2): 185–91.

Mertens, D. M. and A. T. Wilson (2019), *Program Evaluation Theory and Practice*, 2nd ed., New York: Guilford Press.

Miles, M. B. and A. M. Huberman (1994), *Qualitative Data Analysis: An Expanded Sourcebook*, Thousand Oaks, CA: Sage.

Miller, R. L. (2020), *Reducing Stigma and Discrimination in Access to HIV Health Care for Gay and Bisexual Men and Transgender Women Using Mystery Patients in Cameroon and Zimbabwe*, East Lansing, MI: Michigan State University.

Molina-Azorin, J. G. and M. D. Fetters (2018), "Future special issues at *The Journal of Mixed Methods Research*," *Journal of Mixed Methods Research*, 12(4): 369–70.

Moran-Ellis, J., V. Alexander, A. Cronin, M. Dickinson, J. Fielding, J. Sleney and H. Thomas (2006), "Triangulation and integration: Processes, claims and implications," *Qualitative Research*, 6(1): 45–59.

National Commission for the Protection of Human Subjects of Biomedical and Behavioral Research (1978), *The Belmont Report: Ethical Principles and Guidelines for the Protection of Human Subjects of Research* (DHEW Publication No 05-78-0012), Washington, DC: Government Printing Office.

National Ethics Advisory Committee (2019), *National Ethical Standards for Health and Disability Research and Quality Improvement*, Wellington: Ministry of Health. Accessed October 11, 2021. https://neac.health.govt.nz/publications-and-resources/neac-publications/national-ethical-standards-for-health-and-disability-research-and-quality-improvement/

Ozer, E. J. S. Newlan, L. Douglas and E. Hubbard (2013), "'Bounded' empowerment: Analyzing tensions in the practice of youth-led participatory research in Urban public schools," *American Journal of Community Psychology*, 52(1–2): 13–26.

Pahl, R. (1984), "The domestic division of labour between partners," in R. Pahl (Ed.), *Divisions of Labour*, Oxford: Wiley-Blackwell.

Pidgeon, M. (2019), "Moving between theory and practice within an Indigenous research paradigm," *Qualitative Research*, 19(4): 418–36. DOI: 10.1177/1468794118781380

Plano Clark, V. L. and N. V. Ivankova (2016), *Mixed Methods Research*, Thousand Oaks, CA: Sage.

Plano Clark, V. L., K. Schumacher, C. West, J. Edrington, L. B. Dunn, A. Harzstark, M. Melisko, M. W. Rabow, P. S. Swift and C. Miaskowski (2013), "Practices for embedding an interpretive qualitative approach within a randomized clinical trial," *Journal of Mixed Methods Research*, 7(3): 219–42.

Pohatu, P. and T. A. Warmenhoven (2007), "Set the overgrowth alight and the new shoots will spring forth," *ALTERnative*, Special Supplement, 109–27.

Preissle, J., R. M. Glover-Kudon, E. A. Rohan, J. E. Boehm and A. DeGroff (2015), "Putting ethics on the mixed methods map," in S. Hesse-Biber and R. B. Johnson (Eds.), *The Oxford Handbook of Multimethod and Mixed Methods Research Inquiry*, 144–63, Oxford, UK: Oxford University Press.

Rees-Evans, D. and D. J. Pevalin (2017), "Using principle based model to improve well-being in school: A mixed methods pilot study," *SAGE Open*, April–June 2017: 1–9. DOI: 10.1177/2158244017716217

Riha, J., C. Abreu Lopes, N. A. Ibrahim and S. Srinivasan (2021), "Media and digital technologies for mixed methods research in public health emergencies such as COVID-19: Lessons learned from using interactive radio–SMS for social research in Somalia," *Journal of Mixed Methods Research*, 15(3): 304–26. DOI: doi.org/10.1177/1558689820986748

Robinson, C. C., B. Mandleco and S. F. Olsen (2001), "The parenting styles and dimensions questionnaire (PSDQ)," in B. F. Perlmutter, J. Touliatos and G. W. Holden (Eds.), *Handbook of Family Measurement Techniques*, 3, 319–21, Thousand Oaks, CA: Sage.

Shannon, J., A. Borron, H. Kurtz and A. Weaver (2021), "Re-envisioning emergency food systems using photovoice and concept mapping," *Journal of Mixed Methods Research*, 15(1): 114–37.

Shim, M., B. Johnson, J. Bradt and S. Gasson (2021), "A mixed methods-grounded theory design for producing more refined theoretical models," *Journal of Mixed Methods Research*, 15(1): 61–86.

Smith, L. T. (2012), *Decolonizing Methodologies: Research and Indigenous Peoples*, 2nd ed., New York, NY: Zed Books.

Stern, C., L. Lizarondo, J. Carrier, C. Godfrey, K. Rieger, S. Salmond, J. Apo'stolo, P. Kirkpatrick and H. Loveday (2020), "Methodological guidance for the conduct of mixed methods systematic reviews," *JBI Evidence Synthesis*, 18(10): 2108–18.

Sullivan, M., S. Derrett, C. Paul, C. Beaver and H. Stace (2014), "Using mixed methods to build research capacity within the spinal cord injured population on New Zealand," *Journal of Mixed Methods Research*, 8(3): 2340244.

Sweetman, D., M. Badiee and J. W. Creswell (2010), "Use of the transformative framework in mixed methods studies," *Qualitative Inquiry*, 16(6): 441–54.

Tang, J. J., S. Leka and S. MacLennan (2013), "The psychosocial work environment and mental health of teachers: A comparative study between the United Kingdom and Hong Kong," *International Archives of Occupational and Environmental Health*, 86: 657–66.

Tashakkori, A. and C. Teddlie (Eds.) (2003), *SAGE Handbook of Mixed Methods in Social and Behavioral Research*, Thousand Oaks, CA: Sage.

Tashakkori, A., R. B. Johnson and C. Teddlie (2021), *Foundations of Mixed Methods Research*, 2nd ed., Thousand Oaks, CA: Sage.

TDR (2021), About us. Accessed October 29, 2021. https://tdr.who.int/about-us

Teddlie, C. and A. Tashakkori (2003), "Major issues and controversies in the use of mixed methods in the social and behavioral sciences," in A. Tashakkori and C. Teddlie (Eds.), *SAGE Handbook of Mixed Methods in Social and Behavioral Research*, 3–50, Thousand Oaks, CA: Sage.

Thambinathan, V. and E. A. Kinsella (2021), "Decolonizing methodologies in qualitative research: Creating spaces for transformative praxis," *International Journal of Qualitative Methods*, 20: 1–9. DOI: 10.1177/16094069211014766

Titze, K. and U. Lehmkuhl (2010), "Der Elternbildfragebogen für Kinder und Jugendliche (EBF-KJ)]," *Diagnostica*, 52(2): 68–81.

Upadhyaya, M., M. May and L. Highfield (2015), "Integrating classroom, community, mixed methods research, and community-based participatory research to teach public health practice," *Public Health Reports*, 130 (May/June): 286–92.

USAID (2013), *Technical Note: Conducting Mixed-Methods Evaluations*, Washington, DC: Author. Accessed October 29, 2021. https://usaidlearninglab.org/sites/default/files/resource/files/Mixed_Methods_Evaluations_Technical_Note_final_2013_06.pdf

White, H. (2013), "The use of mixed methods in randomized control trials," *Mixed Methods and Credibility of Evidence in Evaluation, New Directions in Evaluation*, 138, 61–73.

Wilson, M. and F. Cram (2018), "Predictive modelling in child welfare – A feasibility study," in M. Tolich and C. Davidson (Eds.), *Social science research in New Zealand*, 233–48, Auckland: Auckland University Press.

Winn, L. T. and M. T. Winn (2016), "We want this to be owned by you: The promise and perils of youth participatory action research," in S. Green, K. J. Burker and M. K. McKenna (Eds.), *Youth Voices, Public Spaces, and Civic Engagement*, 111–30, New York: Routledge.

Wolfe, S. M., A. W. Price and K. K. Brown (Eds.) (2020), "Evaluating Community Coalitions and Collaboratives," *New Directions for Evaluation*, (165). DOI: 10.1002/ev.20400

World Medical Association (2013), *Declaration of Helsinki*, Seoul, South Korea: World Medical Association General Assembly. http://www.wman.net/en/30pubications/10policies/b3/

INDEX